Joseph Agar Beet

The Credentials of the Gospel

A Statement of the Reason of the Christian Hope

Joseph Agar Beet

The Credentials of the Gospel
A Statement of the Reason of the Christian Hope

ISBN/EAN: 9783337022938

Printed in Europe, USA, Canada, Australia, Japan

Cover: Foto ©Lupo / pixelio.de

More available books at **www.hansebooks.com**

THE CREDENTIALS OF THE GOSPEL

A Statement of the Reason of the Christian Hope

BEING THE

NINETEENTH FERNLEY LECTURE

DELIVERED IN CARVER STREET CHAPEL, SHEFFIELD
ON MONDAY EVENING, 5TH AUGUST 1889

BY JOSEPH AGAR BEET

"That thou mightest know the certainty concerning the things wherein thou wast instructed."—St. LUKE

"Ready always to give answer to every man that asketh you a reason concerning the hope that is in you."—St. PETER

Sixth Thousand

LONDON
WESLEYAN METHODIST BOOK-ROOM,
2, CASTLE STREET, CITY ROAD, E.C.;
AND 66, PATERNOSTER ROW, E.C.
1895

PREFACE.

THE following lecture differs somewhat from other statements of the evidences of Christianity by its fuller exposition of the contents of the Gospel of Christ as the matter to be proved. It thus encroaches upon the domain of Systematic Theology. But this encroachment was to me inevitable. For the peculiar contents of the Gospel make needful peculiar attestation. Consequently, according to our conception of the Gospel will be our demand for proof that it is true and our estimate of the validity of such proof.

This exposition of the contents of the Gospel has enabled me to show the bearing of its credentials upon Christian life and especially upon personal assurance of salvation.

I have also endeavoured to distinguish between proof that the Gospel is true, which is the aim of this lecture, and the Authority of Holy Scripture, which is not needful to my argument and with which I have not attempted to deal. This distinction, often overlooked, is of the utmost importance.

My vast obligations to the many writers in this important department of Theology, I can neither acknowledge nor estimate. From them probably has been learnt everything good in this volume. My earliest teachers were Butler and Paley. The famous *Analogy* is still a valued text-book in the schools of Theology, and an abiding power among the many phases of modern religious thought. And, although later Biblical research and modern modes of attack have made needful other works which have somewhat superseded those of Paley, he will ever hold his place of honour as a great leader in the historical attestation of the Gospel.

Among recent works I may mention as of special value, *The Gospel of the Resurrection* by Westcott, *The Basis of Faith* by Conder, *The Foundations of Faith* by Wace, *The Resurrection of our Lord* by Milligan, and *Christian Evidences viewed in relation to Modern Thought* by Row; also by this last writer a very excellent and attractive book of small size and price entitled *A Manual of Christian Evidences*.

Of the contribution to this subject which I now venture to give, the part most needing further development is the argument for the existence of God. But it seemed to me best, in the small space at my command, to discuss fully only one line of evidence, this being itself sufficient proof that the Gospel is true, referring to others merely as they lead up to this chief argument. A good popular book on the topic so scantily treated by me is the *First Principles of Faith* by Marshall Randles.

As a very able and attractive, and within its limits complete, exposition of a subject which I have placed at the beginning of my argument, and which must ever be the foundation both of personal religion and of all satisfactory proof that the Gospel is true, I commend very cordially the Fernley Lecture of last year on *The Christian Conscience* by my colleague W. T. Davison. The brilliant lecture of the preceding year by Dallinger on *The Creator and what we may know of the Method of Creation* anticipated some of the remarks in my section on the Evidence afforded by the Material World. Other statements in the same section have been anticipated in W. Arthur's most able lecture on *The Physical and Moral Law.* Thus it has been my good fortune to build upon a foundation well laid by my predecessors.

Since this lecture was written I have read with much interest a most admirable volume, just published, on *Darwinism* by Dr. A. R. Wallace, a naturalist of the first rank. With great pleasure I notice that he has, by anticipating it, confirmed, even in its spiritual significance, the main argument of Section iii. of this lecture.

The prominence given to Haeckel, some of whose scientific opinions are already discredited, may seem to be beyond his merits. My chief reason for quoting him is that the theological teaching woven into his works on natural science seems to me to be the necessary logical result of modern scientific Agnosticism. Moreover, Spencer and Haeckel are the two authorities on Biology quoted by Huxley in his article on that subject in the

Encyclopædia Britannica. And I do not know of any protest by Agnostics against Haeckel's theological principles. Teaching practically the same as his has lately been set forth with great confidence in a popular form by Clodd. Haeckel, therefore, seemed to me the best representative of theological opinions prevalent now in certain circles, and in their tendency exceedingly hurtful.

These opinions I have endeavoured to combat, not so much by direct disproof, as by plain statement of the Reason of the Christian Hope.

WESLEYAN COLLEGE, RICHMOND.
   9th September 1889.

OUTLINE OF THE ARGUMENT.

SECTION I.

INTRODUCTORY.

	PAGE
The Question before us. Its infinite importance	9
Method of research, and sources of information	11
Practical use of our inquiry	12

SECTION II.

THE EVIDENCE WITHIN.

Moral judgments. Some of these are infallible	13
They imply a standard within us yet beyond our control	14
No mere re-echo of human legislation	ibid.
This standard is universal. Proofs from ancient literature. Testimony of St. Paul. Unconscious testimony of Darwin	15
It is a voice from beyond the frontiers of the material universe	20
It is to us an absolute authority. Yet our moral judgments are not always correct	21
By this standard even the Gospel must be judged	22
The judgment is decisive. The highest in us bows to a greater than itself	ibid.
Dignity of the moral teaching of the New Testament	23
The Old Testament. Other moral teachers	24
The moral teaching of the New Testament is embodied in the character of Christ	25
Supreme authority of this example	27
This lofty ideal reveals our own sin	28
Man's self-condemnation reveals his freedom	29

A

	PAGE
And this is confirmed by the moral helpfulness of righteous self-condemnation	31
Yet human life is under the reign of law	32
Wide-spread conviction that punishment will follow sin	ibid.
This conviction is only partly confirmed by retribution in the present life	34
The imperfect retribution here reveals a retribution beyond the grave. Plato; Buddhist teaching; transmigration	35
Review of our position. We lie helpless under the penalty and the power of sin	37
The sequence of sin and bondage	39
The Gospel of Christ	41
He confirms much earlier teaching;	ibid.
But goes beyond it by proclaiming the salvation we need	42
His transcendent claims, and asserted resurrection	43
If all this be true, our need is supplied	44
The fitness of the Gospel to our need is strong presumption of its truth	45
Results gained. Need for further research	ibid.

SECTION III.

THE EVIDENCE IN THE MATERIAL WORLD.

The observed sequences and co-existences of the material world	48
Two closely-related uses of the word *law*	ibid
In each sense man is under law	49
Natural forces may be diverted in their operation	50
We must therefore endeavour to understand them	ibid.
Are they guided by an intelligent hand?	51
How are they related to the Moral Law?	ibid.
The Lifeless, the Living, the Rational	52
The broad gulf between the irrational and the rational	ibid.
Yet their bodies are closely related	53
The impassable line between the lifeless and the living: chemical constituents, organization, nutrition	54
The crystal: a contrast	56
The forces of inorganic matter operate also in living bodies	57

	PAGE
The geological history of our planet. Strata and fossils	58
The lifeless world, and the gradual development of life	59
The beginning of movement, and the dawn of life, on earth	*ibid.*
How came life to be? By no force now observed in operation	61
Haeckel's attempt to explain the origin of life	63
Its complete failure	64
His dogmatic bias	65
Herbert Spencer's omission	67
The origin of life reveals a power higher than those of nature	*ibid.*
This is confirmed by our study of the moral sense	68
Wide-spread belief in an intelligent Creator. Plato, Cicero	69
Results of our study	71
No relief yet from the penalty and power of sin	72

SECTION IV.

CHRISTIANITY COMPARED WITH OTHER RELIGIONS

Religion is a conspicuous feature of human life, and a marked distinction between man and brutes	74
Elements common to all religions	75
Unique superiority of Christianity	*ibid.*
Immense superiority of Christian nations in political and military power, in art, science, and literature	76
Yet these do not owe their birth to Christianity	77
But they have passed into the hands of Christians	78
Sustained progress of Christian nations	79
Their moral progress	80
This monopoly of sustained progress demands explanation	*ibid.*
It is not set aside by the unbelief of individuals, or by the divisions of Christians	81
No explanation of it except in Christianity itself	83
Rise of Christianity out of Judaism	85
Superiority, and yet comparative weakness, of the religion of Ancient Israel	*ibid.*
Sudden and wonderful rise of Christianity	86
The rise and early decadence of Mohammedanism. The Jews	87
Christianity has saved the world	88

SECTION V.

CHRIST AND THE CHRISTIAN DOCUMENTS.

	PAGE
The strength of Christianity must be sought in Christ	90
Our knowledge of Him is derived from early documents	91
The Epistles of Paul reflect his conception of Christ. They reveal also the writer's intellectual and moral worth	92
The Epistle to the Romans. Justification through Faith. The faith of Abraham	93
Paul taught that God receives into His favour all who believe the Gospel	97
Another type of teaching in the Gospel and First Epistle of John. Its substantial agreement, under different phraseology, with the teaching of Paul	98
Another type of teaching in the First Gospel, and in the Epistle of James. Its agreement with the teaching of Paul	99
The above agreement proves that this doctrine was actually taught by Christ	100
All New Testament writers teach that God frowns on all sin. Moral importance of this teaching	101
Paul taught conspicuously that salvation comes through the death of Christ	102
Similar teaching in all four Gospels	103
Paul taught also that to all believers God gives His Holy Spirit to be in them the animating principle of a new life	104
Similar teaching in the Gospels, and in the Book of Acts	105
The documents examined prove that all these doctrines were actually taught by Christ	106
We have seen that, if true, they will supply our spiritual need	*ibid.*
We therefore ask, With what authority did Christ announce this Gospel of salvation, and how came Paul to accept His word as decisive?	107
Paul's profound reverence for Christ. Unique grandeur ascribed to Him in the Epistles of Paul	108
In each of the four Gospels, this grandeur is reported to have been claimed by Christ	109

	PAGE
The agreement of all the documents proves that this report is correct	110
This claim was conceded to Christ by the Apostles, in spite of His death, because they believed that He had risen from the dead	111
Proofs of this belief, from the Epistles of Paul	*ibid.*
These proofs imply belief in a bodily resurrection	112
Other similar proofs in 1 Peter, Acts, and the four Gospels	113
Indisputably, the immediate followers of Christ believed that God raised Him from the dead in order to prove that He was what He claimed to be	114
This belief explains their profound reverence for Him	*ibid.*
Review. The position gained. Our method strictly historic	115
These claims are unique	116
No such dignity claimed by, or for, Mohammed	*ibid.*
The claims of Buddha. The story of his death	*ibid.*

SECTION VI.

THE HISTORICAL ARGUMENT.

Restatement of the question, and recapitulation of facts adduced. The issues at stake. Did Christ actually rise from the dead?	119
The danger of prejudice	120
Rumoured resurrection of John the Baptist	121
If Christ rose, the courage of the Apostles and the early spread of Christianity are explained; but not otherwise	122
The enemies of Christ had strong reason to dispel the belief that He rose. That they were unable to do so, is strong presumption that the belief was true	123
So is the conversion of Paul	125
The strongest historical argument. If Christ did not rise, the greatest delusion ever known has saved the world	*ibid.*
If so, at the supreme crisis of the world's history, error has been better than truth	126
Then truth no longer deserves man's loyalty	128

	PAGE
The case of Joan of Arc no parallel. Nor Mohammed, nor Buddha. For of all these the strength lay, not in error, but in truth. The teaching of these last needed no miraculous confirmation	128
Consequences involved in denial of the resurrection of Christ	129

SECTION VII.

OBJECTIONS.

Since the above argument does not rest on the infallibility of the Bible, it is not invalidated by any apparent inaccuracies even in the narratives of the resurrection	131
Still less is it weakened by statements not in harmony with modern science,	133
Or by the defective moral tone of a few passages in the Old Testament	ibid.
A more serious objection. "Miracles do not happen." They are inconsistent with the uniformity of nature	134
This objection implies that that which does not happen now never happened	135
It is disproved by the origin of life	ibid.
Close parallel between the origin of life and the origin of Christianity. In each case a new force began to operate in the midst of already existing forces, modifying their operation, and creating a new era	136
Other new eras, revealing the advent of new forces: the origin of motion, and the origin of reason and the moral sense,	139
The rarity of such eras demands in each case careful scrutiny,	140
Successive epochs need cause no surprise	141
We may fairly claim full proof that Christ has risen; but we have no right to deny it beforehand as impossible	142
The slow progress of Christianity is explained by man's freedom, which God gave, and respects	ibid.
Slow development of spiritual life in the Old Covenant; and the slower development of vegetable and animal life	144
Deep underlying harmony of the Christian documents and the Book of Nature	ibid.

SECTION VIII.

THE RESULT.

	PAGE
We accept the Gospel as we accept gravitation, because it is the only conceivable explanation of innumerable phenomena	146
The Christian Faith stated	147
It explains the facts of human life	148
The only alternative is impossible	149
Still stronger proof. Many have dared to believe the Gospel, and have thereby received a moral life which is to them of infinite value. Thus the Gospel is daily verified	150
Each man finds evidence corresponding to his own mental development	151
Practical Results. Deliverance from condemnation and from moral bondage, and a well-grounded personal hope of blessedness beyond the grave	152
Just as our planet is closely linked to, though separated from, the universe of stars, so is life on earth now seen to be one with eternal life	153

NOTES.

I. THE ORIGIN OF THE MORAL SENSE.

Evolutionary Ethics of Darwin and Spencer	155
Serious objections	156
Spencer's gross oversight of an essential distinction	158

II. FREEDOM OR NECESSITY.

The Philosophical Necessity of Mill and Spencer	159
Absence of proof. Serious objections	162
Martineau on the foreknowledge of God	164

III. SCIENTIFIC AGNOSTICISM.

Explanation of the term	164
Darwin's admitted Agnosticism	165
Spencer's Agnosticism. His theory of the universe	166
Haeckel's similar theory	169
Clodd's *Story of Creation*	172
These theories fail to account for the origin of life, for the unique distinction of right and wrong, for man's helpful sense of freedom, and for the history and present position of Christianity	175
Yet they contain valuable elements of truth	177
Services rendered by Scientific Agnostics	178

IV. THE BIBLE AND SCIENCE.

No right to expect in the Bible scientific exactness	179
Remarkable coincidences between Genesis and Science. The Rig-Veda	180
The creation of the stars. Important lesson	183
Silence of science about matters man greatly needs to know	185
The death of animals and of Adam	186
The story of the Flood	187

V. BIBLICAL RATIONALISM.

Relation of Agnosticism to Rationalism	188
Pfleiderer denies the possibility of miracles, and endeavours without them to account for the origin of Christianity	189
Keim's theory recognises a supernatural revelation; but is inadequate	195
Graetz' *History of the Jews*	197
Serious objections to the Rationalistic hypothesis	198
Services to Christian Truth rendered by Biblical Rationalists	199

THE CREDENTIALS OF THE GOSPEL.

SECTION I.

INTRODUCTORY.

THE Gospel is the Good News announced by Jesus of Nazareth. Unquestionably, as we shall see, He taught that endless life and infinite blessedness await all those who believe His words and obey His commands. Unquestionably, these glad tidings were believed by thousands who heard them re-echoed from the lips of the immediate followers of Christ. And from His day to our own they have been believed by millions in every land and of every age, rank, and degree of culture. To hosts of weary toilers this Gospel has made the burdens of life to be glad service of a Master in Heaven. In deepest perplexity and sorrow it has been to them the cheerful voice of a Father in Heaven. And in the gloom of the valley of the shadow of death it has been to a multitude which no man can number the Light of eternal Life. I ask now whether this hope, the Christian Hope, rests upon a foundation of truth, or whether it is the baseless fabric of a dream. If the Gospel be true, it is the greatest truth ever grasped by human thought. If it be not true, the Christian Hope is the strangest delusion that ever led astray the erring mind of man. This alternative, the only possible alternative, I purpose in this lecture to discuss.

Our answer to the question before us will determine our conception of the significance and worth of the visible universe, of ourselves, and of human life on earth. If we have no sufficient proof that the Gospel is true, the material world around us and the life we are now living are the only world and the only life of which we have assured knowledge and in which we have a real interest. If so, strange to say, the life we are now living and the world in which we live, our only life and world, will then have for us comparatively little interest. For, even to the most fortunate, the one will soon pass and the other soon vanish from view. And to the mass of mankind the one is dreary drudgery and the other a vale of tears. But, if the Gospel be true, the visible universe is but a beautifully woven veil hiding from us, or rather to the instructed eye revealing, the more wonderful realities beyond; and our present life is but a faint dawn which will brighten into the glory of Eternal Day. Moreover, if, as Christ and all religious teachers of all lands have taught, our actions now determine our relation to the endless life, every act on earth and all the things on earth which bear upon human action are invested with supreme importance. Compared with this importance, the pleasures and pains of the present life sink into insignificance. Results which will survive the stroke of death are the only objects worthy of our serious thought. On the other hand, if the Gospel be not true, or if we have no proof of its truth, the pleasures and pains of the present are, except for the few who will sacrifice themselves for the good of mankind, our only concern. And, if so, we may well ask, in view of the toil and hardship and sorrow of the present life, whether life is worth living. It thus appears that the question before us involves the highest interests of man.

A question so important demands an answer the most careful. Our search for an answer shall be by methods strictly in harmony with the constitution of the human mind and with the laws of human certainty in matters which have not come under our immediate observation. We shall collect from all sources evidence, *i.e.* matters known by direct observation and bearing upon the question before us. These we will carefully sift and compare, grouping them according to their mutual relations, in order thus to grasp their true significance and to reach the principles underlying each group and the great realities underlying the entire phenomena of life. Our only assumptions shall be facts admitted by a practically unanimous consent of all those acquainted with the case. And both assumptions and deductions shall be clearly stated. Our research will thus be both scientific and philosophical.

Our first evidence will be gathered from the inner life of man as known to each one and as laid open to inspection in the literature of the world. This evidence must be tested by the personal consciousness and experience of each inquirer. Our research will thus begin at the foundation and root and source of all religion, viz. the inborn moral sense. We shall then collect further evidence from the manifold objects lifeless and living spread out before our eyes in the gorgeous panorama of the material world. After surveying for a moment this broad field of view, we shall turn to the social life of men and especially to the religions of mankind, to the facts of human life as seen to-day in the nations of the world. Our observations there will prompt historical research touching the evolution of this social life as attested by the annals of our race. And this will lead us to search the Christian documents. Upon this various evidence we shall build up our chief historical argument. Objections both to the proofs adduced and to our inferences from them will next demand attention. Lastly, we shall recapitulate our various arguments, in order thus to feel their combined force, and to appreciate their significance as a whole and their practical bearing upon the infinite interests at stake.

To some good people, our inquiry will seem to be needless. The question I have proposed, they have already answered. And their faith gives to them peace and joy.

But the firmest faith is strengthened by examination of the solid foundation on which it rests. And whatever strengthens our faith enriches our spiritual life. Moreover, seasons of peace are sometimes followed by days and nights of conflict. And he who at his leisure has carefully surveyed the fortress in which he trusts is best prepared to hold it against the assault of foes. Lastly, every Christian is enjoined to be always ready to give answer to every one who asks a reason of the Christian hope. That we may do this to the many honest doubters found everywhere in this age of doubt, it is most important that we study well the ground of our own faith.

SECTION II.

THE EVIDENCE WITHIN.

We frequently find ourselves pronouncing judgment on the actions and characters of men around us. And the judgments thus pronounced differ in kind and differ infinitely from all others. Material objects, we judge according to their utility or pleasantness to ourselves or to others, and on no other grounds. These considerations influence also our judgments about actions and persons. But about these last, thoughts of utility or pleasantness occupy only a subordinate place. Frequently we give our highest commendation to actions which seem to be neither pleasant nor useful. The difference between the two classes of judgments is also revealed by the different emotions evoked in us by a great calamity and a great crime. To compare these, we feel to be degrading. They belong, as we at once recognise, to different realms of thought and life.

Not unfrequently our judgments about actions and characters, our moral judgments as they are usually called, are pronounced, even in view of human fallibility and error, with a confidence which admits of no doubt and tolerates no appeal. We refuse to discuss whether or not a man who has deliberately and without provocation killed his mother is a villain of very deep dye. When the facts are established, we pronounce with unerring certainty what we know to be a just judgment. Or rather, the only open question is the degree of aggravation of guilt. With similar confidence, every voice within us bears unanimous witness to the nobility of some other actions and characters. Between these limits, and reaching from one to the other by imperceptible gradations, are actions and characters open to more or less doubt. But these gradations and doubts by no means and in no degree lessen the confidence with which we pronounce judgment in extreme cases. Here then, amid many uncertainties we have a secure platform from which we can pursue further inquiry.

These confident judgments imply an infallible standard of comparison. And it is at once evident that this standard is not under our own control. For we cannot change it at will; but are compelled, like judges in our Courts of Law, to decide all cases brought before us on lines already laid down. Many actions, we have no choice but to condemn, sometimes most reluctantly; and others to approve. Not unfrequently we are compelled to pronounce judgment against ourselves. And we then cringe condemned and powerless in the presence of a judge whom we carry in our hearts, but over whom we have no control and from whose sentence there is neither appeal nor escape.

This judge within is no mere re-echo of human legislation. For at his bar must all national laws be themselves judged. Not unfrequently we find ourselves asserting, with a confidence which admits of no doubt, that certain laws are just; and occasionally that some others are unjust. And even in these cases utility is by no means the only or chief ground of our approval or condemnation.

We feel that above the greatest good of the greatest number there is an eternal law of right to which human laws must conform under penalty of being condemned as legalised unrighteousness.

We notice also that in all extreme cases the same actions are approved and the same actions condemned in all nations and ages. The intermediate gradations, especially those far from the extremes, are differently judged, not only in different ages and nations but by different men in the same age and nation. Even in the same person matured thought will often modify in the course of years the standard of judgment in details. But in spite of all this, to speak generally, we find underlying the judgments of every age and nation the same broad principles of morality. All men everywhere know, in spite possibly of their own denial, that treachery, lying, theft, adultery, and murder are condemned by a law which speaks with an unerring voice of indisputable authority.

Of this last statement we have abundant and easily accessible proof. Our best witnesses are not modern travellers and missionaries; or even modern heathens. For every converted or unconverted heathen describing to Christians the state of his countrymen is more or less influenced by those to whom he speaks. And, naturally, converted heathens, looking back upon their heathenism, can hardly avoid exaggerating the darkness from which the light of the Gospel has rescued them. A surer testimony is found in the literature of the ancient world. In its pages the hearts of men who lived and thought long before Christ was born and far from the voice of Sinai lie open without reserve to our inspection. This gives to the classic writings of Greece and Rome unspeakable value. And their witness is confirmed by the Sacred Books of the East, which year by year are being brought, in good translations, within our reach.

These many and various and widely separated witnesses testify with one voice that the broad principles of morality which determine our judgments to-day also underlay the entire thought and life of the ancient world. To reproduce, in a few pages, the force of this unanimous testimony, is impossible. It is found not so much in single sentences as in the entire tone of the early literature of the world. But it may be illustrated by a few quotations.

SOPHOCLES, the great Athenian tragic poet, in his drama of *Oedipus the King*, lines 863–71, represents a chorus of Theban old men as bursting into song, in reply to the queen, who had set at naught a prophecy of Apollo, with these words, " May destiny still find me winning the praise of reverent purity in all words and deeds sanctioned by those laws of range sublime, called into life throughout the high clear heaven, whose father is Olympus alone; their parent was no race of mortal men, no, nor shall oblivion ever lay them to sleep; the god is mighty in them, and he grows not old." We have here clear consciousness of a standard of right independent of man and abiding for ever.

Similarly, the same writer in his *Antigoné*, lines 449–60, represents Creon king of Thebes as saying, " And didst thou dare to transgress that law ? " and Antigoné as replying, " Yes; for it was not Zeus that had published me that Edict; not such are the laws set among men by the Justice who dwells with the gods below (*i.e.* ruling the dead); nor deemed I that the decrees were of such force that a mortal could override the unwritten and unfailing statutes of heaven. For their life is not of to-day or yesterday, but from all time, and no man knows when they were first put forth. Not through dread of any human pride could I answer (*i.e.* pay penalty) to the gods for breaking these." It is true that the law disobeyed by Antigoné was only one forbidding the burial of her brother. But her language reveals the poet's deep consciousness that above all human laws are other laws claiming, apart from or in spite of human laws, and under penalty of punishment, absolute obedience.

XENOPHON, the Athenian historian, in his *Memoirs of Socrates*, bk. iv. 4, 19-21, records a conversation of Socrates with Hippias to the following effect: "Dost thou know, said he, Hippias, any unwritten laws? Those in every country, said he, held binding touching the same things. Wouldst thou then be able to say, said he, that men made them? Why how, said he, could all men come together when they do not speak the same language? Then who do you suppose, said he, has made these laws? I think, said he, that gods gave these laws to men. For with all men it is thought right first of all to reverence gods. Is it then everywhere thought right to honour parents? It is, said he. Also that parents and children do not marry? To me, Socrates, this does not seem to be a law of God. Why? said he. Because I see some, said he, transgressing it. Yes, and many other things they do against law. But then they who transgress the laws made by the gods pay a penalty which in no way man can escape; just as some who transgress laws made by men escape punishment, secretly or by violence."

DEMOSTHENES, in his oration *On the Crown*, p. 317, says: "And not only will these principles be found in the enactments of the law, but even nature herself has laid them down in her unwritten laws and in the moral constitutions of men." We have here an express acknowledgment of a superhuman law.

From Greece we turn to Rome. In CICERO'S work *On Laws*, bk. ii. 4, we read: "This, then, as it appears to me, has been the decision of the wisest philosophers,—that law was neither a thing contrived by the genius of man, nor established by any decree of the people, but a certain eternal principle, which governs the entire universe, wisely commanding what is right and forbidding what is wrong. Therefore they called that primal and supreme call the mind of God enjoining or forbidding each separate thing in accordance with reason. On which account it is that this law, which the gods have bestowed on the human race, is so justly praised. For it is the reason and mind of a wise Being equally able to urge us to good and to deter us from evil. . . . . For even he (Tarquin) had the light of reason deduced from the nature of things, which incites to good actions and dissuades from evil ones; and which does not begin for the first time to be a law when it is drawn up in writing, but from the first moment that it exists: and its existence is coeval with the divine mind. Therefore the true and supreme law, whose commands and prohibitions are equally authoritative, is the right reason of the Sovereign Jupiter."

The above quotations might be multiplied indefinitely. They are confirmed by the entire literature of the ancient world.

Our list of witnesses shall be closed by the words of a Christian teacher. In Romans ii. 14, 15, the Apostle Paul writes: "Whenever Gentiles, the men who have no law do by nature the things of the Law, these, having no law, are to themselves a law; inasmuch as such men show the work of the Law written in their hearts, while their conscience bears joint witness to the same, as do their reasonings one with another accusing or excusing." He means that the occasional performance by the heathen, apart from external influences, of the actions prescribed in the Law of Moses proves that their own moral nature is to them what the Book is to Israel. And this assertion he supports by saying that their obedience, however imperfect and fragmentary, reveals the conduct prescribed in the Law of Moses inwoven into the texture of their moral nature; and that the inward faculty by which a man contemplates and estimates his own action confirms the testimony given by their occasional right conduct, as do also their thoughts and words when condemning or excusing one another. Of such reasonings by heathens about the conduct of themselves and others, and of their consciousness of an inner law written upon their hearts, the above quotations are good examples. Apart from the authority of Holy Scripture, these words of St. Paul are of immense value as the testimony of a keen observer of the heathen world.

The unanimous testimony of ancient writers is confirmed by not a few moderns who are unable confidently to accept the Gospel as true. In vol. i. of the *Life and Letters of Charles Darwin*, p. 307, we find a letter in which, replying to a correspondent, the great naturalist confesses his complete uncertainty about even the existence of a personal Creator, and yet adds that in spite of this uncertainty "man can do his duty." This reveals his consciousness that, apart altogether from the historical truth of Christianity, for each man and known to each, there is a marked-out path along which he is bound to walk. And of such testimonies the writings of modern Agnostics are full.

It is true that Darwin, and others still more confidently, suggest that our sense of moral obligation has been evolved out of man's bodily needs taken in connexion with his material and social surroundings; or, in other words, that the moral sense is an outworking of forces operating before human life began. But even these teachers assert that, apart from all thought of consequences, certain actions we know to be right and others wrong, and that we are bound, with an obligation inexplicable but peremptory, to do right and to avoid wrong.

This unwritten yet deeply-written inner law and the imperative obligation to obey it are phenomena demanding explanation. They are absolutely certain. And not only are they coextensive with human life and history but they occupy a far higher level of importance than do all the phenomena of the material world taken together. A noble action and a noble man are grander far than all material grandeur. We honour a man who prefers to die rather than do a shameful act. And in our heart of hearts we feel that his stern resolve is an inspiration of highest wisdom. This supreme importance of morality and the inborn standard of moral judgment are facts demanding explanation. They cannot be classed under any of the sequences observed in the visible world around us or explained by any of the forces at work in it. Therefore, like all unexplained phenomena, they reveal the existence of forces other than these. They are voices speaking to us from beyond the limits of the material universe and bearing witness to a universe beyond. In other words, while listening to the voice within we stand on the borderland of a world unseen and profoundly mysterious, yet both near and real and of supreme importance. No philosophy of life and of the universe can satisfy us or gain our respect unless it do something to explain these phenomena so far-reaching, so important, and so mysterious.[1]

The significance of the evidence now adduced, we will consider at a later stage of our inquiry. In passing we notice that in all ages and nations the moral standard within has been accepted as the voice of a personal authority beyond and above the visible universe and claiming to rule the conduct of men. Of this wide-spread belief, the quotations above furnish examples. Others innumerable might be added.

Whatever be the source of moral distinctions, we are compelled to admit that the moral standard written within is the highest authority in human life and thought. In the solitude of our own spirit, far from the tumult of the world around, it speaks to us with a voice we cannot gainsay. Without contradiction it is to us the court of ultimate appeal. We know that to obey it is for our highest welfare, that to disobey it is to trample under foot that in us which is noblest and best. And, stranger still, we know that, apart from all thought of our own

---

[1] See Note i., on The Origin of the Moral Sense.

welfare, we are bound at all hazards to do right and to avoid wrong.

When speaking of the authority of the moral sense, we must carefully guard against seeming to say that our moral judgments are always correct. This is by no means true. But when our judgments are given with confidence, as is often the case, they are absolutely binding upon us. And not unfrequently we know that our judgment is infallibly correct. Of such infallible judgment we have already given an example.

To the mysterious tribunal within appeals all external teaching moral and religious. And by the arbitrament of the Judge there enthroned must all such teaching be judged. The teaching of Jesus is no exception. We wait with intense interest to hear the verdict and sentence on the Gospel of Christ pronounced by this unerring Judge.

The judgment is decisive. The moral teaching of the New Testament commends itself at once and irresistibly to our own moral sense as right and good. It does more than this. The teaching of Christ and His Apostles not only appeals to, but raises and strengthens, the standard within. It sets before us a clearer and loftier conception of right and of the beauty of right, and a nobler ideal of human excellence than we had before; and gives to this ideal a mightier authority. And this effect continues and increases from day to day. In our best moments we turn to the recorded words of Christ; and never in vain. As we reverently study them, we rise into and breathe a clearer and purer moral atmosphere. At the voice which speaks to us from the pages of the New Testament, the Judge within, himself our lord, bows as in the presence of

One Greater than himself. Or, rather, henceforth his rule over us is strengthened by the external authority to which he bows. In other words, the New Testament commends itself to us as loftier and better than that in us which is loftiest and best. A voice which does this wields an authority we cannot gainsay.

As examples of the moral teaching of the New Testament, I may mention the two great commandments quoted from the Old Testament in Matt. xxii. 37–40: "Thou shalt love the Lord thy God with all thy heart and with all thy soul and with all thy mind. This is the great and first commandment. And a second is like it: Thou shall love thy neighbour as thyself. On these two commandments all the Law hangs, and the prophets." Also the precept of Christ in Matt. v. 44, 45: "Love your enemies and pray for those who persecute you; that ye may become sons of your Father in Heaven: for He maketh His sun to rise on bad men and good, and sendeth rain upon just men and unjust." We feel at once the grandeur of a morality which rises above the little details of mere prescription and sums up man's whole duty in love to God and love to man; and which takes as a pattern of universal beneficence binding upon all men the undistinguishing kindness of the God of Nature. A world in which these precepts were obeyed would be more like Heaven than earth. And in proportion as we obey them do we attain real moral excellence.

Quotation, however, cannot reproduce the moral authority of the New Testament. This can be felt only by personal study. It is attested by not a few who, while rejecting as untrue many of its historic statements, give to the New

Testament as a whole, because of its moral teaching, the first place in the literature of the world.

It is right to say that here and there in the Old Testament we find passages which do not commend themselves to our moral sense, and which therefore have for us no moral authority. As examples I may quote the commendation in the song of Deborah (Judg. v.) of Jael's treachery; and the vindictive language in Ps. cxxxvii. 9. But we notice that such language is found only in the literature of the Old Covenant which was professedly preparatory and imperfect. Everything in the New Testament commands our highest respect. Even in the Old Testament such language is rare. For the more part, its moral teaching not only claims our respect but raises our moral ideal. Indeed the two great precepts quoted above from recorded words of Christ were quoted by Him from the Old Testament. The moral superiority of the Jewish Scriptures becomes very conspicuous when they are compared with any other sacred books of the ancient world.

It is also right to say that much other literature besides the Bible makes a similar appeal to our moral sense and therefore speaks to us with similar authority. This is true even of non-Christian writers, especially ancient writers. And it must be at once admitted that all such writings claim irresistible authority over us. They are, especially to those who have never heard anything better, the authoritative voice of God. For whatever commends itself to us as good becomes an obligatory rule of conduct. Fortunately, between these various teachers there is little collision. What the New Testament approves as good and condemns as bad is approved and condemned by the general consent of the moral teachers of all nations and ages.

That in non-Christian literature moral teaching which we are compelled to accept as good is sometimes associated with historic statements which we cannot accept as true, warns us that the moral authority of the Bible is not, taken by itself, complete proof of its historic truthfulness. The historical statements of the Bible, some of which are of immense importance, must be submitted to the scrutiny of historical criticism. This scrutiny, in reference to the most important of these statements, will occupy our attention at a later stage of our investigation.

Whatever the New Testament teaches about moral excellence is presented to us realised in actual human life in the character of Jesus of Nazareth. Every moral excellence is but a feature in His portrait. So wonderful is the influence of this picture that we tolerate in Christ with reverence, as befitting the majesty of Him who condescends to speak to us, assumptions which from any other we should reject with indignation. The Carpenter declares[1] that He alone knows God and can reveal God to men, that[2] all earlier teachers were thieves and robbers, that[3] He is the only way to God, and that they who have seen Him have seen God and need not ask for any other vision. He offers[4] rest to the burdened and weary by laying upon them His yoke. Yet, while making these unheard of assumptions, He calls Himself meek and lowly of heart. And, strange to say, we feel that these words

---

[1] Matt. xi. 27.
[2] John x. 8.
[3] John xiv. 6, 9.
[4] Matt. xi. 28, 29.

are true. Compare these claims with those of any other teacher. Comparison is impossible. He spoke as man never spoke before.

The claims of Jesus were greater even than these. In the New Testament, as we shall see in Section v., He claims to be immeasurably greater than the greatest of men, occupying a unique relation to God which He describes by calling Himself the Master's Son, whereas all others are but servants. He asserts that He was with God before the world was; and that He will return to be the Judge of all men. He allows to go without contradiction an accusation of His enemies that He claimed to be equal to God. No similar assertions made by a living man touching himself are recorded in the literature of the world.[1]

But it is not the majesty of Christ as He is portrayed in the New Testament which moves us most. It is rather the wonderful condescension of One so great. We see Him possessing infinite power, yet coming down to the level of human weakness in order to rescue the helpless; veiling His glory in human flesh that it may not blind us but may be to us the light of life. We see infinite resources used, never to gratify or exalt their possessor, but only and without reserve for the good of others. In Him we see, as His disciples understood Him, God becoming, in all points except sin, like man, in order that in all points except deity men might become like God. We see Him living a human life on earth of which every thought, word, act was obedience to God and goodwill to men. As the

---

[1] See in Sec. v. the assertions about himself said to have been made by Buddha.

one return for this infinite love and self-sacrifice He claims from His followers unreserved loyalty to Himself and to the good of the race. In the hearts of thousands, the love of Christ to man has evoked a devotion never before given by man to man; and has been a powerful motive for all that is pure and right and good. Call this if you will, or can, the dream of admiring followers. A dream like this man never dreamed till Christ appeared. And, dream or no dream, it appeals to our highest moral sense as the noblest ideal of excellence and the strongest motive to virtue we can conceive. Judged by the infallible standard within, it is the brightest light we have ever seen.

The portrait of Jesus claims at once supreme authority over us. And this claim is absolute, even apart from the historic truthfulness of the picture. For, whatever we know to be good, we are bound to do under penalty of condemnation by the Judge within. Moreover, the example set before us is suitable for all persons in all positions and at all times. Unfavourable circumstances cannot prevent us from doing to others as we would they should do to us, and from loving God with all our heart and our neighbour as ourselves. Consequently, circumstances cannot excuse us from obeying the commands, and imitating the example, of Christ. And the universal applicability of the example increases its authority. For it both leaves us without excuse, and is a proof of the superhuman origin of the example. In the new light which has fallen upon us we are compelled to judge ourselves and others.

We have now observed in our own inner life two important phenomena, viz. the supreme authority of our own moral sense, and the homage paid by our moral sense to the teaching and example of Christ. To these must at once be added another closely-allied phenomenon.

The lofty moral ideal presented to us reveals not only our own littleness but our sin. The brightness of the vision which shines upon us from the pages of the New Testament brings to light our own deep pollution, and our actual transgressions. In that light we see how far and how inexcusably we have fallen below our privilege and duty.

This effect of the exhibition of moral beauty has been often attested. By giving greater definiteness to the law written within, external precept or example has aroused a sense of personal sin. Many such testimonies are found in the Bible, which apart from any special divine authority is indisputably a correct transcript of the inner life of men. In the light of a vision of the Holy One of Israel described in Isa. vi., the prophet cries: "Woe is me! for I am undone; because I am a man of unclean lips, and I dwell in the midst of a people of unclean lips: for mine eyes have seen the King, the Lord of Hosts." And in chapter xlii. 5, 6, Job says: "I had heard of Thee by the hearing of the ear; but now mine eye seeth Thee. Wherefore I abhor myself, and repent in dust and ashes." A remarkable example is found in Luke v. 8, where, without any moral teaching and prompted only by demonstration of the supernatural power of Christ, Peter cries: "Depart from me; for I am a sinful man, O Lord." This consciousness of personal sin and sinfulness, evoked by a sense of the nearness of God, is a marked feature of the sacred literature of ancient Israel. And the words there used have been found by the best men of all Christian nations to be a suitable expression of their own deepest thoughts.

Not unfrequently, the shining forth of new moral light has quickened memory and illuminated forgotten pages of the past. This has been in all ages illustrated by the effect of powerful preaching. Under searching moral appeals, and still oftener under vivid delineations of the mercy of God in Christ—and His mercy is a revelation of moral grandeur—men have confessed unsuspected crimes. For in the light which shone around them their guilt could find no hiding-place.

Stranger still, this clearer moral light reveals frequently the inexcusableness of sins committed before the light came. This has often been noticed on the mission field when the Gospel has been preached to men who never heard it before. And the reason is plain. Every moral voice from without awakens a forgotten voice within.

Abundant testimony to the wide-spread consciousness of personal sin might be quoted. Many who to others seemed blameless have, in the secret chamber of their own hearts, been covered with confusion at their own shortcomings. But in the matter before us testimony is needless, and useless. Each must pronounce judgment on himself. Any one who is unconscious of personal sin lies outside the scope of the Gospel. But his unconsciousness of sin does nothing whatever to lighten the condemnation which by their own confession rests on many others. To these only pertains our present inquiry.

From the consciousness of personal sin, and from the condemnation we have frequently been compelled to pronounce against ourselves and others, flows directly a consciousness of personal freedom. By this I mean a conviction we cannot shake off that our evil actions, even when suggested and stimulated by influences from without, were not inevitable sequences of these influences, but that in each case the ultimate decision to yield or not to yield was with ourselves, and with ourselves alone.

Very often we have striven hard to escape self-condemnation by tracing our actions to irresistible influences which left us no choice. And in proportion to the success of these efforts we have silenced the judge within. But again and again our efforts have been in vain; and we have stood condemned and ashamed before a tribunal from which there was no escape and in presence of sins which claimed us as their author. Our inmost consciousness has told us that we were free. Similarly, our condemnation of others is always in inverse proportion to the strength of the influences under which they acted. In other words, our moral judgments imply that men are free, that it rests with themselves alone to yield to or resist the influences leading them towards sin. A consciousness of personal freedom is inwoven into the deepest tissues of human thought and moulds all our judgments about ourselves and others.

The strength of this conviction is itself a presumption of its truth. For it is in the last degree unlikely that the confident and universal thought of man about man in all ages should be a delusion.

This sense of freedom is not contradicted by our observation that all sin robs the sinner in some measure of his moral freedom, and that our past actions are a present power drawing us to-day along the path we trod yesterday

For our bondage is a consequence and punishment of our own past sins; and therefore has its real source in ourselves. But we have no proof that the accumulated present power of our past sins is irresistible. If we thought so, we should surrender ourselves, in moments of severe temptation, as morally lost. That sometimes men who have fallen far and foully strive bravely to retrieve themselves, reveals their conviction that freedom is not absolutely lost even by deep sin: and their moral victory, even when imperfect, is a strong presumption that their conviction is true.

Once more. Our inability to ascribe our sins to irresistible influences acting upon us to-day or moulding our disposition in days gone by has often been in a very high degree morally helpful to us. As we have been compelled to look in the face our own bad acts, we have firmly resolved to avoid in the future the sins we have committed in the past. And, in spite of the weakness and frequent failure of human purposes, we have found this resolve and the bitterness of our self-condemnation to be a powerful deterrent from sin. Consequently, whatever dispels our sense of freedom breaks down a great bulwark of morality. Whoever, therefore, teaches that all human action is an inevitable sequence of certain antecedents existing before the actor was born works injury to men. Is it conceivable that that which is morally hurtful can be actually true? If so, truth itself has become the abiding foe of man. For the moral phenomena now before us are not small, or transitory, or local, but as important, as abiding, as widespread as human life. If on a scale so vast delusion were helpful, and knowledge injurious, to man's highest interests, then ignorance is practically better than knowledge and error better than truth. Against a doctrine involving consequences so tremendous I must in the name of science and philosophy utter my loudest protest. For both science and philosophy rest upon the assumption that knowledge is for the good of man.

Man is free, the ultimate author of his own actions and the supreme arbiter of his own fate. But he is none the less under the absolute reign of law. Moving among inevitable moral sequences which he did not make and from which he cannot escape, he nevertheless chooses his own steps and thus determines his own destiny. If so, there are in human life three chief factors; influences from without antecedent to or simultaneous with personal action, free choice, and the inevitable results, material and moral, of man's free choice. To all these, witness is borne by human consciousness. And the witness is true.

The above assertion and proof of man's moral freedom is not essential to my present argument that the Gospel is true. But the importance of it, and the injuriousness and the prevalence in certain quarters of the opposite error, led me while speaking of man's self-condemnation to note this inevitable and serious inference from it.[1]

Clearly associated with the unique and authoritative distinction of right and wrong and our felt obligation to do right and refrain from wrong, and with the wide-spread consciousness of personal sin, is an equally wide-spread conviction that on the one hand sin and punishment and on the other hand virtue and happiness are linked together by an inevitable sequence which has its root in the nature

[1] See Note ii.

of man and in the whole realm of things around him. We cannot shake off our conviction that sooner or later the sinner will have to reckon with his own sins. And this fear of punishment, cast aside in the moment of sin, returns in more thoughtful moments and is itself a beginning of punishment.

To this apprehension of punishment inevitably following sin, the entire literature of the world bears witness. It breathes throughout the poetry and philosophy of ancient Greece. As a good example I may quote Xenophon's *Anabasis*, bk. ii. 5. 7, 8, where a Greek commander says to a Persian general: "First and chiefly, the oaths of the gods forbid us to be hostile one to the other. And whoever is conscious of having disregarded these, that man I should never esteem happy. For I know not with what kind of speed and whither fleeing one would escape the hostility of the gods. For all things everywhere are subject to the gods, and everywhere equally they are masters of all things." Here we have one heathen reasoning with another, a stranger in race and religion, on the ground of broad principles recognised by all nations. And similar examples are abundant.

The above reference to the gods implies that in the speaker's thought the sequence of sin and punishment had a superhuman source.

Exact retribution inevitably following all actions good and bad is taught constantly and is everywhere implied throughout the sacred books of India, Brahmanical and Buddhist. To these books I shall shortly refer again.

This sequence of sin and punishment, of virtue and happiness, is on the whole confirmed by our observation of human life around us. But the retribution we see now is far from perfect. To speak generally, right doing brings in the long-run visible benefit, and wrong doing sorrow, to the actor. And when this is so, our moral sense experiences a sort of satisfaction. We feel instinctively that retribution is as it should be. This sense of satisfaction is in part explained, and is certainly strengthened, by the evident benefit which the right action of each brings to the race as a whole. But this is by no means a complete explanation. Apart from visible results, the majesty of right claims from us absolute loyalty. And we cannot shake off a conviction that this claim is supported by a power able to reward and to punish.

Nevertheless, not unfrequently we notice that the good man suffers because he is good, and that others escape death and obtain material wealth because they are worthless. In other words, judging from what falls under our observation, the sequence of action and retribution seems to be again and again broken.

This imperfection of apparent retribution in human life on earth has in all ages perplexed the minds of men. In coarser minds it has had the effect of obscuring, though it could not altogether hide, the visible majesty of the moral law and the inevitable sequence of sin and punishment. Some have attempted to explain it by saying that virtue is its own reward and vice its own punishment. But this explanation breaks down utterly in the case of a man who has lost his life by doing a noble action. For him there is no reward, even for the highest virtue, in the present life. And the best men may be objects of our pity. This cannot be. We feel instinctively that they are objects, not of pity, but of emulation. Another explanation must be sought.

It has been found. In all ages of the world and in all nations, among the most cultivated and among some very barbarous, the inequality of moral retribution in the present life has been explained by a belief that the present life is not the whole case, that the balance of retribution due at the moment of death is carried forward into an existence beyond the grave, and that in other worlds there is absolute recompense.

To give examples of this almost universal belief, may seem to be needless. As a representative of ancient Greek thought I may quote Plato's greatest work, *The Republic*. In bk. x. pp. 612-4, he says, "The nature both of just and unjust is truly known to the gods? Granted. And if they are both known to them, one must be the friend and the other the enemy of the gods, as we admitted at first? True. And the friend of the gods may be supposed to receive from them every good, except only such evil as is the necessary consequence of former sins?" Note here the inevitable sequence, in spite of the friendship of the gods, of sin and punishment. "Certainly. This then must be our notion of the just man, that even when he is in poverty, or any other seeming misfortune, all things will in the end work together for good to him in life and death: for the gods have a care of any one whose desire is to become just and to be like God, as far as man can attain the divine likeness, by the pursuit of virtue?" Plato, or Socrates who is supposed to be speaking, then shows that even in the present life, ultimately, virtue brings reward and vice punishment. He adds, "These then are the prizes and rewards and gifts which are bestowed upon the just by gods and men in the present life, in addition to other good things which justice of herself provides. Yes, he said; and they are fair and lasting. And yet, I said, all these things are as nothing either in number or greatness in comparison with those other recompenses which await both just and unjust after death." He then tells a story [1] of a vision of judgment beyond the grave, where the dead receive tenfold good or bad in proportion to their actions on earth.

Absolute retribution, beginning in this life and completed beyond the grave, permeates the entire religious thought, ancient and modern, of the Hindus and the Buddhists. As one out of innumerable examples, I may quote the beginning of the *Dhammapada*, a work of the Buddhist canon: "All that we are is the result of what we have thought: it is founded on our thoughts, it is made up of our thoughts. If a man speaks or acts with an evil thought, pain follows him as the wheel follows the foot of the ox that draws the carriage. . . . If a man speaks or acts with a pure thought, happiness follows him like a shadow that never leaves him." Further on we read: "The evil-doer suffers in this world, and he suffers in the next; he suffers in both. He suffers when he thinks of the evil he has done; he suffers more when going on the evil path. The virtuous man is happy in this world and he is happy in the next."

This wide-spread conviction of the inevitable sequence of sin and sorrow is further attested by the strange belief, found in the writings of Plato and in the ancient though

---

[1] Appropriately quoted by Davison. *Christian Conscience*, p. 113.

not in the oldest writings of India, and continuing to our day among the Hindus and Buddhists, that the living have lived on earth before they were born and that the vast majority of them will live again after they are dead, and that the ills which in the present life come to a man without his own desert are punishments for sins committed in a former life. So strong is the conviction, in Indian thought, that sin and sorrow are linked together by an indissoluble tie that, in order to explain suffering inherited by birth or not merited in the present life by the sufferer, the Hindu has invented a previous existence which has left no trace whatever in the memory of man. Than this strange belief, held to-day by many millions in India and China, there can be no clearer witness to man's deep sense of the moral inequalities of the present life on earth and of the felt need of complete retribution.

All religions proclaim rewards and punishments beyond the grave. And doubtless to this important element of truth the various religions of the world owe, in great part, their hold upon the hearts and minds of men. For they thus appeal to man's inborn sense of the supreme majesty of Right and of the essential evil of sin. This appeal has supported their authority even where the worship of the gods has been degraded by foolish superstitions and by tolerance of gross sin. The plain proclamation of a judgment to come has been a great element of strength in the teaching of Mohammed. And the still clearer moral teaching of the New Testament has in all ages exalted the authority of the Gospel of Christ.

Let us now, in view of the foregoing facts, consider our position. In our hearts we carry a Judge from whose voice of authority there is no appeal. By that Judge we stand convicted of many inexcusable sins. Moreover, thus convicted, we cannot throw off a dark foreboding that sin will be followed by punishment. And, since we see no adequate retribution on earth, we are compelled to believe that retribution awaits us elsewhere. Day by day our weary feet are treading a path which leads to the dark river of death and towards the unknown land beyond. And as our eyes strive to pierce the darkness of that silent shore, our hearts are troubled by memories of innumerable sins which fill us with sad forebodings. Vainly we listen for a voice from beyond the flood announcing to us a way of safety.

No mere moral teaching can save us; not even the lofty morality quoted on p. 23 from the lips of Christ. For such teaching only tells us what we must do in order to obtain the rewards of virtue. And even the Sermon on the Mount threatens punishment to all who do wrong. We have again and again done what we knew to be wrong; and we dread the penalty of our sins. From that penalty, only pardon can save us. And, of pardon, the moral law knows nothing.

Only one resource remains. We will learn wisdom from our failures in the past; and in future we will resolutely turn from all sin, and do only what we believe to be right. Or, rather, we will walk in the steps of the great moral Teacher who speaks to us from the pages of the New Testament, and endeavour to realise the ideal He has set before us. Yet, even then, we cannot expect that future obedience will break the mysterious link which binds together our past sins and their due recompense. But we may hope that in the inevitable retribution which awaits us future right doing may be set against past wrong doing, and thus mitigate our punishment. Such is our resolve.

Strange to say, this good resolve does but reveal the hopelessness of our position. For we find ourselves utterly powerless to accomplish it. And this discovery reveals the presence in our hearts of an almost irresistible foe forcing us along the path of sin. In proportion to the keenness of our moral sense and the earnestness of our moral efforts is our consciousness of moral bondage. Against the hostile power within we struggle with only occasional success. Again and again we are forced downwards along the steep descent of sin.

It is now evident that we need deliverance not only from the future penalty of our past sins but from their present power; or, in other words, that the sins we committed yesterday are a power leading us almost irresistibly to-day along our former path. We have here a second moral sequence. Not only are we unable to shake off a fear of future penalty, but we are conscious of moral weakness resulting from the sins of former days. And this weakness, itself a consequence of sin, increases our fear of further consequences to come. For it shows how utterly sin is opposed to our moral nature.

This second moral sequence, viz. sin and demoralisation, is matter of direct observation. That it is invariable, is attested by our own inner life from the dawn of memory to the present day and by the observed outer life of society around us. No sequence in the material world rests upon more complete evidence. And none is so important. It is a law of our moral nature as invariable as is gravitation in the material universe. And we can no more escape from the operation of the one than of the other. We may break the law which marks out the moral path in which we ought to go. In this respect we are free to do right or wrong. But we cannot break through the law which declares that every sin depraves and enslaves the sinner and that every virtuous act ennobles the actor. We are free to choose our own actions: but the inward and outward results of our actions are determined according to an invariable law. So with the laws of nature. It is ours to observe the material and moral sequences, and so to adapt our conduct as to escape evil and attain the greatest good. Thus under the reign of omnipresent law man is free. Or, rather, he would be free but for his own sin and the consequent moral bondage.

The inward bondage of the sinner to a power against which his good resolves are powerless is abundantly attested in ancient and modern literature. It will be sufficient to quote Euripides, *Medea*, line 1078: "I know what sort of bad things I am going to do: but passion is stronger than my purposes. And this is to mortals a cause of very great evils." So Seneca says in *Letter* 52: "What is it that draws us in one direction while striving to go in another; and impels us towards that which we wish to avoid?" These and many other similar testimonies of heathens are confirmed by the annals of crime in our own day.

And now follows, or would follow but for the light of the Gospel, the gloom of moral despair. And the darkness of that despair will be in proportion to the clearness of our moral vision. No sophistry can persuade us that the voice which commands us to do right is other than the law of our being, or that our presentiment of punishment to follow sin is a delusion. We know that we have sinned, and we dread the consequences. We observe that these consequences do not follow sin in their fulness in the present life: and we therefore are afraid that we shall meet them beyond the grave. Not only so, but we find ourselves powerless to avoid repeating our past sins. And this proves how far we have gone astray.

We need then a double deliverance, viz. from the future penalty of sin, and from its present power. And these must go together. Moreover, no voice of pardon will give us peace unless it be supported by an authority equal to the supreme authority within which condemns us. Nor can we listen for a moment to any pardon which fails to pay homage profound to the majesty of the eternal law of righteousness.

While thus we lie, condemned and helpless, from the pages of the New Testament there comes to us a voice of mercy. Already from those pages, in the moral precepts of Christ, a voice has spoken to us which has been recognised in the tribunal within as having supreme authority. Moreover, in those pages we have seen reflected an ideal of human excellence which has secured the allegiance of whatever in us is noblest and best. And, closely interwoven with this authoritative moral teaching, we shall find other teaching of an altogether different kind. This now demands attention.

As His words are reported in the New Testament, Christ confirmed in many points the teaching prevalent in His own and other nations about the unseen world. He is represented as teaching that beyond and above the visible universe is a universe unseen by men; that above all else reigns One Almighty, All-knowing, and Infinitely Good, the Maker of all things and the loving Father of angels and men; that the law written as we have seen in the hearts of all men is His will touching His intelligent creatures; and that beyond the grave absolute retribution awaits all actions good or bad done on earth. This teaching, if true, explains the moral phenomena noted above, viz. the supreme and unique majesty and the universality and independence of the law written within, man's presentiment of retribution, and the inequality of retribution in the present life. And it is the only conceivable explanation of these wide-spread and all-important phenomena. This is a very strong presumption that the explanation is correct.

We notice, however, that this teaching, common to Christ and in some measure to others before Him, so far from helping us out of the difficulties from which we now seek relief, only increases our sense of the helplessness of our position.

Fortunately, the recorded words of Christ and the writings of His Apostles contain other elements of teaching peculiar to the New Testament; except that anticipations of them more or less definite are found in the Jewish Scriptures. The Prophet of Nazareth is represented as proclaiming eternal life of infinite blessedness for all who believe the good news announced by Him. He recognises the personal guilt of those to whom He promises life, the inviolability of the Law, and the punishment therein threatened to all transgressors. But He points to His own approaching violent death upon the cross as the mysterious means by which sinners are to escape the due penalty of their sins. Yet He declares that God smiles only on those who obey the moral law. And, wonderful to tell, He promises, as no teacher ever promised before, to breathe into His disciples His own Spirit that It may be in them the animating principle of a life like the ideal life He lived on earth, and may impart to them a moral power able to break the fetters which have long held them in bondage. These promises are the distinctive elements of the Gospel of Christ as set forth in the New Testament.

It is at once evident that this Gospel offers to us all we need. To men conscious of innumerable personal and inexcusable sins and unable either to escape from or to endure the inevitable consequences of their sins, Christ announces pardon. To men held fast by the inward bondage of sin, He announces moral liberty. To men sinking into the grave and deeper than the grave, He announces endless life. The completeness of this remedy proves that it comes from a physician who knows man's inward need better than does man himself. And this intimate knowledge is no small presumption that He who knows can heal.

The sufficiency and the grandeur of these promises suggests at once a question about the authority of Him who speaks them. We reverently ask, Who is He, and what right has He thus to speak?

Christ is represented in the New Testament as claiming to be the Only-Begotten Son of God, the future Judge of all men. His immediate disciples believed, as we shall see in Section v., that He was also the Creator of whatever began to be. If this claim be just, and this belief correct, we are satisfied. If the Judge of all men pronounces our pardon, our own moral sense can no longer condemn: for it bows to His authority. He who made us at first can rescue His workmanship even from the mightiest foe.

One more question remains. What proof have we that these stupendous personal claims of Christ are just, that He is what He professed to be? The New Testament furnishes us a reply by asserting that He rose from the dead. If this historic statement be correct, every question is answered and our every need is supplied.

Notice also that nothing less than the above would be a sufficient foundation for intelligent belief of the Gospel. No voice could silence the condemnation pronounced by what we must acknowledge to be the supreme authority within us except the voice of One Greater than man. Nor could we admit the claim of a man, flesh and blood like ourselves, to be infinitely greater than the greatest of men unless there had been manifested in Him a power infinitely beyond all human power. In other words, we have in the account of Christ given in the New Testament, if that account be correct, all that we need for reasonable faith and for complete salvation; and we have nothing more than we need.

Already we have seen that the moral teaching of Christ claims our allegiance with an authority we cannot gainsay. This indisputable authority confirms in no small degree the unique promises so closely interwoven with the moral teaching of Christ. For it is in the last degree unlikely that with such moral light would be associated delusion in matters bearing closely on morals. And this presumption is now raised almost to certainty by the wonderful and exact fitness of the Gospel to supply man's moral and spiritual need.

When we see a complicated key opening at once a very complicated lock, we infer with certainty that lock and key have a common origin. Every one admits that our inference is reasonable. It is based, not simply on the fact that a key opens a lock—for in some cases this would be small proof of common origin—but on the complexity of lock and key which makes accidental agreement inconceivable. So does the Gospel correspond with, and supply, man's deep and manifold need. In neither case can we define exactly the amount of complexity needful for complete conviction. But in each case we are sure that apart from a common or related origin such harmony amid such complexity would be impossible. There are thousands of Christian men who amid the vicissitudes of life find each fresh need supplied by the Gospel of Christ. This is to them complete proof that their own higher nature and the Gospel have the same origin; and that therefore either human life is unreal and worthless or the Gospel is true. To them life is gloriously real. Therefore with unwavering faith, as they bow with profound reverence before the character of Jesus portrayed in the New Testament, they accept as true His teaching as there recorded.

Let us now review again the position gained. We have found in our hearts a standard of right and wrong, of higher and lower, from which in many cases there is no appeal. And in the New Testament we have found moral teaching which by the tribunal within is certified as supremely good; and a sublime portrait of human excellence before which all others fade into insignificance. But that moral splendour only revealed our own deep sin; and awoke in us a dark foreboding of retribution. And, inasmuch as we see no sufficient retribution in the present life, we could not repress an apprehension of retribution beyond the grave. In this fear, the moral teaching and the example of Christ gave us no direct relief. But they stimulated strenuous efforts to do right. Sad to tell, these efforts only revealed our moral weakness and bondage. In our despair there came to us from the pages of the New Testament a voice promising to all who believe this good news superhuman inward power over sin and immortal life. This promise is represented as made by One who claimed to be infinitely greater than the greatest of men, and who in proof of these stupendous claims rose from the dead.

This entire teaching filled us with wonder. If it be true, our dark forebodings are dispelled, and our highest hopes will be more than realised. Nay, more. So wonderful is its completeness, so different from and superior to all other teaching of any age or nation, that even the teaching itself bears evidence on its own front of its unique and superhuman origin. We are certain that a light so glorious was never kindled amid the gloom of earth and in the deluded brain of man. The only possible explanation of the facts of the case is that the Gospel is true.

This very strong presumption is a definite point already gained in our present inquiry.

It is however right to say that the above argument, complete as it is within its own wide limits, is only a general proof of the truth of the teaching of Christ. It is by no means sufficient evidence that all the statements about Christ in the New Testament are true, and that all the teaching there attributed to Him came actually from His lips. On these points we need further and more exact information. What we have already learnt rather quickens than satisfies our inquiry. We shall therefore proceed now to seek in other directions further evidence.

SECTION III

THE EVIDENCE IN THE MATERIAL WORLD.

In our search for further evidence touching the truth of the Gospel of Christ we turn now to the visible universe which like a great illustrated book lies open to our view.

Already in the inner life of men we have noticed invariable sequences, especially the inevitable sequence of wrong doing and moral degradation. And in the course of human life we have noticed a sequence, general though apparently not uniform and adequate, of sin and sorrow. We now notice in the material world an immense variety of other invariable sequences and co-existences. So invariable are many of these that frequently one observed phenomenon gives us complete assurance of the existence of another; and from a known event we infer confidently certain antecedents and certain consequences. Many of these sequences we notice to be linked together by a chain which we speak of as causality. So manifestly real is this link of cause and effect that we conceive a mysterious something underlying it which we call force.

Generalisations of these observed sequences are called the Laws of Nature.

Notice carefully two distinct uses of the word *law*. It denotes always a delineation of action, or at least of movement. But the Moral Law and the laws of nations describe a path along which men ought to go. The Laws of Nature describe invariable sequences of certain antecedent conditions; or in other words the path along which natural forces actually operate.[1]

The relation between these two very different kinds of law is much closer than at first sight appears. National laws declare the punishment which will follow crime; and thus delineate the action of the government towards criminals. And the Moral Law, which lays obligation upon those under its sway, is supported by an observed and very subtle moral sequence which has its root deep down in the foundation of human nature and which links together with an indissoluble tie sin and degradation and sorrow. On the other hand, the Laws of Nature may be obeyed or disobeyed. For we may so adapt our action as to obtain from their operation many benefits; or from failure so to do we may lose property, health, and life. These consequences may be not unreasonably called the rewards and punishments attached by Nature to her own Laws.

Amid this similarity there is however a radical difference. Our condemnation of a man who breaks the moral law differs in kind from our judgment of one who fails to take care of himself by adapting his action to the laws of nature. The latter is a mistake; the former, a sin.

In a double sense, then, man is under law. He is surrounded by sequences he cannot break through: and he has received commands which he knows that he is bound

---

[1] See Arthur's very able Fernley Lecture on the *Difference between Physical and Moral Law.*

to obey. Nevertheless, he is free. For he may so act that the inevitable sequences bring him weal, or woe. And he may obey or disobey the Law written within. To adapt his action to the one and to obey the other, is the condition of human welfare. For life ever demands, for its well-being and continuance, adaptation to its environment.

We notice that frequently one natural force is apparently neutralised, and is certainly diverted from its path, by other forces. Especially we notice that natural forces are diverted by the intelligent action of men. For instance, we hold up a weight which otherwise would fall to the ground. In this case the force of gravitation is diverted in its operation. But it is by no means suspended. That it operates still, and in full measure, the sensory nerves of the arm bear indisputable witness. On the other hand, the avalanche rushes on in a resistless and merciless course. But even in this and similar cases man often escapes by flight. Not unfrequently, however, this is impossible. And we perish crushed in the iron grasp of forces we cannot withstand. Very mysterious forces are ever operating in our bodies. The effect of these we may in some measure modify for a time and thus guard our health and lengthen life. But in spite of all that we can do they are driving us irresistibly to the cold embrace of death.

Inasmuch as man's well-being depends upon his self-adaption to his environment, a knowledge of the environing forces becomes of the highest interest to him. We ask, therefore, whence comes the universe around us of which ourselves form a part, and whence came the mysterious laws interwoven in strange complexity and underlying the observed sequences of the material and the moral world? Sometimes the forces of the material world seem to be both blind and deaf. For they have no pitying eyes for the terrible sorrow they inflict and are apparently deaf to the shrieks of their victims. With profound anxiety we ask, Are the inevitable sequences which hold us in their firm grasp and threaten to crush us a mere outworking of blind natural forces; or is their uniform action designed, guided and controlled by a supreme intelligence? Or, in other words, Are we at the mercy of brute force infinitely inferior to ourselves, or are we in the hands of an all-seeing and omnipotent Father?

Already we have found in the universal moral sense of men, and in the felt majesty of the Moral Law, influences real and powerful which cannot be classed under the far-reaching forces observed at work in the material world. We have also noticed invariable moral sequences operating in the inner life of man and far more important than the forces of the material world. And in the incomplete retribution of our present life on earth we have found a strong presumption that the present life is only a part of a larger whole, and that human intelligence will survive the stroke of death. These phenomena we could not explain by any of the forces known to be at work in matter. From this we inferred the existence of some force or Agent other than the forces of the material world. The supreme importance of moral phenomena suggests very strongly that such Agent must be not only different from, but superior to, the forces immediately underlying material phenomena.

We now ask, What light is cast upon this suggestion by the phenomena observed in the world around us? Can these be explained by the forces now observed operating in matter? Or does the material world, like the moral sense of man, itself bear witness to the existence and operation of forces other than the forces of nature?

We notice at once that the objects around us are divided by a broad demarcation into lifeless, living, and rational. From certain points of view, the boundaries of these categories seem almost to touch. The monera lie near to the boundary line of lifeless and living; and the highest apes are not very far removed in bodily form from the lowest savages. But more careful examination reveals, between each of these classes, an infinite gulf.

From the highest apes the lowest savages differ in the possession of a spoken language, in the use of fire, in the cooking of food, in the manufacture of weapons, and in dress. Interesting and abundant proof of this is given in a work edited by Herbert Spencer and entitled *Descriptive Sociology*. And this difference places an infinite distance between monkeys and savages.

A difference still more marked is seen in the capacity of even the lowest savages to be raised by contact with civilisation and religion. A conspicuous instance of this is found in the Fuegians seen by Darwin on his voyage in the *Beagle* and mentioned on page 618 of his work on *The Descent of Man*. In his later days the great naturalist expressed his wonder and delight at the success of missionaries in raising these degraded savages. In vol. i. p. 264 of his *Life and Letters*, we read: "It is admirable to behold what the missionaries both here and in

New Zealand have effected. I firmly believe that they are good men working for a good cause. I much suspect that those who have abused or sneered at the missionaries, have generally been such as were not very anxious to find the natives moral and intelligent beings." Again, in vol. iii. p. 127, he writes: "I had never heard a word about the success of the T. del Fuego mission. It is most wonderful, and shames me, as I always prophesied utter failure. It is a grand success. I shall feel proud if your Committee think fit to elect me an honorary member of your Society." Between the religious education imparted by these missionaries and the highest training possible to animals, how vast the difference! This difference reveals the infinite distance between man and brutes. No one ever dreamed of a mission to monkeys. For the highest animals lie outside and beneath the great brotherhood which includes the whole human race.

This broad mental and moral difference is by no means inconsistent with the close relationship of the bodies of men and animals. Of this we have abundant proof. Nor does it contradict the hypothesis that man's body was descended from irrational ancestors. And undoubtedly many, or nearly all, living forms have been modified by the interaction of heredity and the influence of environment. But no laws of animal development can account for the unique intelligence and moral sense of man. If man's body has been evolved from some humbler form, we must conceive that, when the bodily evolution was complete, a higher life from a loftier source was breathed into the fully developed form. Be this as it may, man's unique intelligence and moral sense reveals the operation of a force or agent higher than the influences at work in the animal world.

Still less open to question is the line which separates the living from the lifeless. Living bodies are marked off from the lifeless by a mysterious faculty of appropriating internally to themselves other matter in the form of food and by their need of food for a continuance of their normal state; by their faculty of propagating their kind; and by a capacity for movements different in kind from those caused by mechanical contact or chemical affinity or an electric current. With the possible exception of the very lowest forms of life, living bodies differ from those which have never lived by their remarkable structure as seen under the microscope. And they differ from all bodies which have no connexion with life by their absolutely unique chemical composition.

These differences demand further attention. We begin with the last. All living or once-living bodies consist of very complex combinations never found except in connexion with life but made up of some four or six chemical elements found abundantly, in simpler combinations, in inorganic substances. I refer to the mysterious carbon compounds of Organic Chemistry. The abiding association of these elements, in the proportions and peculiar forms found in living or once-living bodies, cannot with any probability be accounted for by the laws of chemical affinity or of any known forces operating in inorganic bodies. And when life departs, except under very unusual circumstances, these unstable combinations begin, in all bodies in which the phenomena of life are conspicuous, at once to break up, and their elements to re-arrange themselves in simpler combinations. This is the cause of the corruption of dead matter. Thus the chemical constitution of living bodies, inexplicable by chemical affinities only, reveals the operation of a force differing in kind from the known forces at work in inorganic matter.

Not less peculiar is the structure of living bodies as revealed by the microscope. To use a well-known illustration, every living body (except the simplest which consist of only one cell) is a republic of minute cells, each possessing a certain completeness and independence of its own. With the exception of the lowest form of life, lately discovered, each cell contains within itself a smaller body, the *nucleus*, which seems to be the inmost seat of life. Nothing similar to this is found in inorganic bodies. Nor do we ever find in inorganic bodies any tendency to form either a cell or a nucleus.

Not less distinctive is the faculty of living bodies to appropriate to themselves other bodies in the form of food, *i.e.* to inweave them into their own structure and thus to grow. Vegetables appropriate to themselves elements which have not necessarily any previous connexion with life. They feed on inorganic matter. Animal life can be maintained, except perhaps in those lowest forms which lie as debatable ground between the animal and vegetable kingdoms, only by consuming that which itself has had life. Nutrition, and growth by means of nutrition, are common to all living bodies, and are never found elsewhere.

Closely allied to growth is the faculty of living bodies to propagate their kind.

These contrasts and their combined significance will become still more conspicuous if we compare with them that form of inorganic body which most nearly approaches living bodies, the crystal. The great difference between the flat hard surface and the sharp and regular angles of the one and the soft and rounded form of the other at once attracts attention. We notice also that crystallization, mysterious as it is, does not require or produce any new chemical combination; and therefore does nothing to explain the unique chemical combination of all living bodies, a combination which while it lasts is altogether inexplicable by the laws of chemical affinity. In crystals, the microscope reveals no cells and nuclei, or anything bearing the slightest resemblance to them. It is true that the crystal grows as the saturated solution evaporates. But it grows by the addition of new particles to the outside. It never receives, as do all living bodies, such particles into its interior. Moreover, living bodies require for a continued exhibition of the phenomena of life, a constant reception into themselves of new matter from without. Of nutrition in any form, the crystal is independent.

Such then is the broad demarcation between the living and that which has never lived. A sort of borderland between them is occupied by that which has lived and lost its life. And in this borderland are a large number of very complex chemical combinations such as are never found except in some association with life. Some of these have been produced by the combining skill of man. But, apart from life, they are never found in nature. And their elements are ever ready to break up and re-arrange themselves in simpler combinations.

It is, however, right to say that inorganic and organic

bodies are most closely related. The forces which operate in lifeless matter operate also in living bodies. For instance, these last obey and in a measure are controlled by the force of gravitation, sometimes to their destruction. At other times they seem to set it at nought, as when we leap from the ground, or hold up an object which otherwise would fall. But this apparent defiance is in appearance only. Gravitation operates with undiminished force. But, instead of carrying the body to the ground, it produces weariness in the arm which holds it. In other words, it is diverted from its course by the presence of life; and, like a rebounding ball, pursues its path in another direction. Similarly, chemical forces also are at work in living bodies: and their operation is needful for life. A living body is a wonderful laboratory in which chemical processes, caused by chemical affinities and needful for maintenance of life, are ever taking place. When life has ceased, chemical forces dissolve the body and reduce it to dust. In other words, inorganic bodies are governed simply and only by certain forces operating throughout the visible universe. In living bodies these forces also operate. But their operation is modified and their course diverted by the presence of other forces peculiar to life.

Matter once living but now dead is under the domain of the laws of inorganic matter. But some of the results of life continue in chemical combinations always associated with life yet surviving it for a time and giving rise in the process of dissolution, under the influence of chemical affinities, to phenomena peculiar to dead bodies.

Keeping in view this threefold division of objects around us into lifeless, living, rational, we now turn to read the history of man and of life as written in plain letters upon the rocks beneath our feet.

One glance at a quarry reveals to us layers of rocks lying one upon another. And as we pass from place to place we notice a marked difference in colour and general appearance between rocks in different parts of the country. More careful observation tells that, like the small beds of rock visible in quarries, also these great formations of different kinds of rock, though of immense thickness, follow a definite succession of higher and lower, each coming to the surface like edges of the bent back leaves of a book. And it is impossible to doubt that these various stratified rocks were deposited in the same way as to-day deposits are forming at the mouths of rivers and elsewhere; and that therefore the various formations mark successive eras of the ancient history of our planet. To this silent narrative of the past, so wonderfully preserved for us and lying open for our study, we now turn for further light upon the matters before us.

The rocky pages of the great book are illustrated by numberless pictures taken from life and presenting the forms of plants and animals which once grew and breathed. We soon notice that these pictures vary with the various formations of rocks. They tell us the story of the earth before men began to live.

A slight perusal of these ancient documents assures us beyond a shadow of doubt that the world was not always as it is now; that long before man trod its soil there were upon it quadrupeds, some of gigantic size; that earlier still were great reptiles, and before these fishes; and that the world itself, and probably some rocks now existing, are older than the earliest forms of life.

It is also evident that the simplest forms of life, animal and vegetable, were the earliest. As we turn over the pages of the record we notice that in successive ages higher forms appear. The geological era of life has been conveniently divided into five periods, which may be roughly described by saying that in the earliest and lowest we find sea-weeds and invertebrate animals; in the next ferns and fishes; in a third pines and reptiles; in the fourth forest trees and mammals; in the latest cultivation and man. It is also evident that each successive period has been shorter than the preceding one.

Ascending now the stream of time, through the above successive epochs, we reach at last the earliest dawn of life. There must have been a time when life, a very lowly form of life, probably the lowest, began to be. Wonderful moment. Hitherto the only forces operating on earth have been those inherent in matter, such as gravitation, chemical affinity, electricity, etc., together with a mysterious impulse acting upon matter from without and in a direction different from that of the inherent forces, and disturbing the equilibrium towards which these forces ever tend. Some such impulse there must have been. And it may be said to have created motion. With it time began. But now appear upon the scene new phenomena revealing a force unknown before and creating another era in the history of our planet. Particles of carbon, oxygen, nitrogen, hydrogen, with one or two other elements, break loose from the stable chemical combinations in which they have hitherto been held together; and, following a new and incomprehensible attraction, arrange themselves in combinations unknown before, combinations which cannot be explained by the chemical forces which have hitherto been omnipotent. Other wonders still more wonderful await the gaze of whoever then had eyes to see. The new chemical combinations assume new outward forms. Within a small mass of what has till now been homogeneous matter is evolved a nucleus: the first step in the long path of organization. Into the now living organism particles of inorganic matter are drawn, and are changed by strange alchemy into the composition and nature of the absorbing body. It thus grows. The nucleus and the cell divide, forming new cells. These are united into a composite body. In time different cells adapt themselves to their different environments and develop different functions. At last, where once were only wind and wave and subterranean upheaval, we find variously developed and abundant vegetable and animal life.

This is not romance but undoubted fact. It is true that we cannot determine, even in geologic time, when life began. For, probably, or certainly, the earliest forms of life have perished without trace. The softness of their structure doomed them to early destruction. Moreover, the earliest rocks have themselves evidently undergone change. And this might account for the absence of organic forms. But we cannot doubt that there was once a temperature on earth in which life, according to all the known laws of life, was absolutely impossible. At least, not otherwise than by cooling down from intense heat can we conceive the origin of the solar system. If so, since life exists now, and at one time did not exist, there must have been a time when it began to be. And that distant time witnessed the operation of forces new in the history of the world, of forces never seen in operation, and so far as we know never operative, in later ages. For the most careful scrutiny of scientific research has failed to detect the development of life out of lifeless matter.

In the above assertion that our planet was once entirely lifeless, all students of natural science agree. So Haeckel says in vol. i. p. 327 of his *History of Creation*: "We can therefore, from these general outlines of the inorganic history of the earth's crust, deduce the important fact, that at a certain definite time life had its beginning on earth, and that terrestrial organisms did not exist from eternity, but at a certain period came into existence for the first time." This writer I mention specially not only because of his ability but also because I am compelled to combat most strenuously certain theological dogmas interwoven with his attractive scientific teaching. Moreover, in asserting that life on earth began to be he does but express the unanimous opinion of all who have studied the subject.

We now ask, How came life to be? What was the mysterious force, stronger at that point than chemical affinity, which broke up stable combinations, set free their component atoms, drew them together into forms hitherto unknown, and held these forms together in spite of chemical forces tending to dissolve them? Whose was the hand that arranged the newly-combined atoms into cells, concentrating their matter into a nucleus and clothing it with an envelope, that combined the cells into a composite living body, and endowed cells and organism with the functions of life?

It was no hand of nature, as we see nature around us now. It was no force now observed at work in the material world. For the most careful scrutiny, by men of whom some are very eager to find what they seek, has failed to discover in inorganic matter any force tending to draw together the component elements of living bodies, or tending in the least degree to build them up into organized forms. Still less has any one been able to suggest a natural force capable of imparting to lifeless bodies the various properties of life.

That in the present order of the material world life never springs from the lifeless, Huxley asserts in pages 238, 239 (lecture 10) of his *Critiques and Addresses*, and claims as a result of modern scientific research the broad induction that all life is derived from life. In vol. iii. of the *Encyclopædia Britannica*, p. 689, he says, "The fact is, that at the present moment there is not a shadow of trustworthy direct evidence that abiogenesis (the growth of the living out of the lifeless) does take place, or has taken place, within the period during which the existence of life on the globe is recorded. . . . If the hypothesis of evolution is true," as Huxley believes it to be, "living matter must have arisen from non-living matter; for by the hypothesis, the condition of the globe was at one time such that living matter could not have existed in it, life being entirely incompatible with the gaseous state But living matter once originated, there is no necessity for another origination, since the hypothesis postulates the unlimited, though perhaps not indefinite, modifiability of such matter."

It is not too much to say that the derivation of the

living from the lifeless lies altogether outside the capacity of the forces known to be at work now in the material world. It therefore reveals the presence of a power higher than the forces of nature.

This last inference is denied by Haeckel, who asserts that all the phenomena of life can be accounted for by the operation of forces now at work in norganic matter. In his *History of Creation*, vol. i. p. 334, he says, "Modern physiology has arrived at the strictly monistic conviction that all of the vital phenomena, and, above all, the two fundamental phenomena of nutrition and propagation are purely physico-chemical processes, and directly dependent on the material nature of the organism, just as all the physical and chemical qualities of every crystal are determined solely by its material composition. Now, as the elementary substance which determines the peculiar material composition of organisms is carbon, we must ultimately reduce all vital phenomena of nutrition and propagation to the properties of carbon. *The peculiar chemico-physical properties, and especially the semi-fluid state of aggregation, and the easy decomposibility of the exceedingly composite albuminous combinations of carbon, are the mechanical causes of those peculiar phenomena of motion which distinguish organisms from anorgana, and which in a narrow sense are usually called 'life.'*" The italics are Haeckel's.

In ch. xiii. of the same work, the writer endeavours with great skill to show how the outward forms of life might be produced by the operation of the forces now seen at work in inorganic matter. This he does more fully in ch. vi. of his earlier and very able though in this country less known work, *Generelle Morphologie der Organismen.* Indeed Haeckel believes (*History of Creation,* vol. i. p. 344) that " Among the monera at present known there is a species which probably, even now, always comes into existence by spontaneous generation." Unfortunately, the only place suggested as the probable scene of this all-important phenomenon is in mid-ocean from two to five miles beneath the surface of the Atlantic. We have already seen that this belief is said by Huxley to be without " a shadow of trustworthy direct evidence."

The close congruity between the phenomena of life and the chemical constitution of living bodies, I cordially admit. But Haeckel not only fails to show how the constituent elements could assume the outward form of life but also does nothing whatever to show how, apart from pre-existing life, they were brought together. He refers to the formation of crystals as in some sense analogous to the origin of life. But we have already seen (on page 56) that this analogy fails in several all-important points. Moreover crystallization takes place daily before our eyes. Whereas as Haeckel is compelled to admit, the closest scrutiny has failed to detect the transition from lifelessness to life. Scientific research rather affords a presumption that such transition never takes place now. Certainly it has no parallel in the material world so far as it is known to us.

Haeckel reminds us that in recent years some organic combinations have been artificially produced. This merely means that, with great difficulty and by the chemist's skill, elements never found combined in nature in the same proportions have at last been brought together in chemical union. But it does no more to prove that they could have been brought together by the forces at work in inorganic matter than a page of type set up by a compositor does to prove that such a combination of type could be produced by gravitation.

In short, Haeckel does nothing whatever to explain, by the operation of the forces inherent in inorganic matter, the chemical constitution of organic bodies, the origin of organic cells, and the wonderful phenomena of life. Yet life must in days gone by have been developed out of inorganic matter. And this development, so different from all developments now observed, must have had a sufficient cause. That cause, since we cannot find it in inorganic matter, the only form of matter then existing, must have been non-material. In other words, there was once at work on earth a force never seen at work now; or at least a force producing results never produced now. And since the first production of life is infinitely more wonderful than any of the subsequent developments of life, this force must be superior to all natural forces. This assured result of natural science is an important confirmation of the teaching of Christ and of nearly all other religious teachers. For, indisputably and conspicuously, He spoke ever of an Unseen Creator and Ruler of the material world.

The dogmatic and theological bias of Haeckel is not concealed. After suggesting how the earliest living creatures, which not without reason he supposes to have been monera, sprang into life out of lifeless matter which he supposes to have been eternal, he admits on page 340 of vol. i. of his *History of Creation* that such spontaneous generation has never been observed. But on pages 347-49 he goes on to say: "The origin of the first Monera by spontaneous generation appears to us as a simple and necessary event in the process of the development of the earth. We admit that this process, as long as it is not directly observed or repeated by experiment, remains a pure hypothesis. But I must again say that this hypothesis is indispensable for the consistent completion of the non-miraculous history of creation, that it has absolutely nothing forced or miraculous about it, and that certainly it can never be positively refuted. . . . If we do not accept the hypothesis of spontaneous generation, then at this one point of the history of development we must have recourse to the miracle of a *supernatural creation*. The Creator must have created the first organism, or a few first organisms, from which all others are derived, and as such he must have created the simplest Monera, or primæval cytods, and given them the capacity of developing further in a mechanical way. I leave it to each of my readers to choose between this idea and the hypothesis of spontaneous generation. To me the idea that the Creator should have in this one point arbitrarily interfered with the regular process of development of matter, which in all other cases proceeds entirely without his interposition, seems to be just as unsatisfactory to a believing mind as to a scientific intellect." In other words, Haeckel assumes that there is no Creator, or at least that it is inconceivable that He should interfere in nature; and weaves an hypothesis, of which he admits that he has no shadow of proof, to fit in with his theological assumption. Such *à priori* reasoning about a matter which lies outside the material world, with which alone natural science has to do, seems to me most unscientific.

In Herbert Spencer's *Synthethic Philosophy*, a very able attempt to explain, apart from the supernatural, the phenomena of nature, we miss a discussion of the origin of life. This omission is acknowledged in the original prospectus. It is also again referred to in a paper appended to vol. i. of the *Principles of Biology*. Spencer differs somewhat from Haeckel in denying an "absolute commencement of life." He supposes that, under conditions very different from those now existing, inorganic matter passed by insensible gradations into organic matter and into living forms. But all gradations, sensible or insensible, imply a competent force tending in their direction. And, so far as I know, no one has yet detected any force in inorganic matter tending in the direction of organism and life.

In the mysterious origin of life we have now found complete proof that there exists a force other and higher than those at work in inorganic matter. This force must be of a loftier kind than any of its effects; *i.e.* it must be superior to human intelligence. Moreover, the immense importance of life, proportionately insignificant in bulk as it is, to the history of our planet, forbids us to suppose for a moment that the presence of life on earth is a mere accident, an unconscious outworking of blind forces. That results so stupendous should come without design, is more unlikely than that geometrical figures on the sea-shore were produced by the waves. Far easier is the suggestion that the universe and life and reason are the designed outflow of a life and intelligence higher than that of man. The grandeur of the universe points upwards to a source greater than itself.

This result of our observation of the world around

receives strong confirmation from our study in Section ii. of the moral sense. For, like the origin of life, the majesty of the moral sense of man cannot be accounted for by any forces inherent in matter. And so closely is the moral sense inwoven into man's nature, and so close is its relation to his material environment, that when once we admit that both life and the moral sense have a supernatural source we cannot doubt that their origin is the same. And it must be superior to the intelligence and the moral sense of man. In other words, beyond and above the forces of nature is an intelligent power which at first produced life and intelligence and which now claims to rule the moral life of all intelligent beings. And, if so, we cannot doubt that He who made all things will vindicate His claim by absolute retribution.

To many persons these inferences receive still further confirmation from the experiences of daily life. They find the world to be a wonderful though rough school of spiritual education. Even the hardships and sorrows of life develop in them endurance, and courage, and confidence in an intelligent Power greater than the forces of nature; and thus reveal man's own superiority to his surroundings. Thus what seem to be the blind forces of nature work out spiritual good. Amid apparent discord there is profound harmony. "To them that love God all things work together, for good." This unexpected harmony cannot be accidental. It bears plain marks of design. Such marks we have already found in the material world looked at by itself. But, when we observe that natural forces are mysterious handmaids leading and helping men to obey the supreme judge enthroned within and thus to gain his approval, the marks of design become such as to banish all doubt. Indisputably the forces of nature and the moral law have the same intelligent Source and are working out the same great Purpose.

That the material universe was made by an intelligent Creator, Himself without beginning, and that man's moral sense is a transcript of His will in the heart of man, has been held firmly in all ages and nations. The most splendid embodiment of this belief which has come down to us from the ancient world is the *Timaeus* of Plato. He declares, on p. 28, that the visible and tangible universe is not eternal but created; and goes on to speak of the Father and Maker of the universe as intelligent and good. He supposes that the Eternal God created first intelligent and superhuman beings, and that these made the material world and man.

Similarly Cicero, at the beginning of bk. ii. of his work *On the Nature of the Gods*, says: " What can be so plain and evident, when we behold the heavens, and contemplate the celestial bodies, as the existence of some supreme, divine intelligence, by which all these things are governed ? Were it otherwise, Ennius would not, with universal approbation, have said,

> 'Look up to the refulgent heaven above,
> Which all men call unanimously Jove.'

This is Jupiter, the governor of the world, who rules all things with his nod, and is, as the same Ennius says, ' Of gods and men the sire,' an omnipresent and omnipotent God. And if any one doubts this, I really do not understand why the same man may not also doubt whether there is a sun or not. For what can possibly be more evident than this? And if it were not a truth universally impressed on the minds of men, the belief in it would never have been so firm; nor would it have been, as it is, increased by length of years, nor would it have gathered strength and stability through every age. And in truth we see that other opinions, being false and groundless, have already fallen into oblivion by lapse of time. Who now believes in Hippocentaurs and Chimeras? Or what old woman is now to be found so weak and ignorant as to stand in fear of those infernal monsters which once so terrified mankind? For time destroys the fictions of error and opinion, while it confirms the determinations of nature and of truth. And therefore it is that, both amongst us and amongst other nations, sacred institutions and the divine worship of the gods have been strengthened and improved from time to time." Cicero quotes, in § 6, Chysippus the Stoic as saying: "If there is anything in the universe which no human reason, ability, or power can make, the being who produced it must certainly be preferable to man. Now celestial bodies, and all those things which proceed in any eternal order, cannot be made by man. The being who made them is therefore preferable to man. What then is that being but God? If there be then no such thing as a Deity, what is there better than man, since he only is possessed of reason, the most excellent of all things? But it is a foolish piece of vanity in man to think that there is nothing preferable to him: there is therefore something preferable: consequently, there is certainly a God."

It is true that Cicero represents the speakers in his dialogue as supporting their belief by some arguments which we should not now consider valid. But the work just quoted affords abundant proof of the wide-spread belief that the world is no product of blind force but the work of an intelligent and eternal Creator.

It is also right to say that the earliest Buddhist writings say nothing about God, and represent Buddha as refusing to discuss the origin of the world.

The wide-spread belief in an intelligent Creator and Ruler of the universe, I mention only in passing. It is no part of my argument. But inasmuch as wide-spread and persistent beliefs are almost always found to contain, even when in part erroneous, important elements of truth which enable them to survive the overthrow of other beliefs, this almost unanimous belief deserves respectful attention. And we have seen that it is confirmed by the inability of modern science to explain, by the known operation of natural forces, the phenomena of life.

Such then are the results of our search in the moral world within us and in the material world around. In our hearts we have heard a voice speaking with an authority to which we are compelled to bow. That voice condemns us: and from its condemnation we find no way of escape. Even our efforts to obey it do but reveal our inward moral bondage. The felt and supreme majesty of the Moral Law itself attests the existence of an authority higher than the greatest on earth. For it cannot be explained by the operation of natural or social forces. We cannot yield to these the homage which we cannot refuse to the Moral Law. Indeed sometimes we feel ourselves bound, in obedience to this supreme authority, to trample under foot every kind of material good. This felt obligation reveals the presence of an authority greater than ourselves and mightier than the irresistible forces of nature. We have also just seen that, apart from moral obligation, the material world itself, and especially the origin of life, bear witness to the existence of a power altogether different from and greater than the forces now seen in operation. For no known natural force does anything whatever to span the gulf between the lifeless and the living. And indisputably that gulf has been spanned. We have also seen that each of these lines of evidence supports the other. This combined evidence is sufficient to prove the existence of an Unseen and Supreme Power.

The grandeur of human life has assured us that it cannot be an outworking of blind forces. The Author of intelligence and of moral sense must Himself be both intelligent and moral. And the universe must be an accomplishment of an intelligent purpose. Thus in the material world we have found footprints of One infinitely greater than man or the world.

It must be admitted with sadness that the evidence just derived from the material world affords no relief from the difficulties laid upon us by the authority of the Moral Law. In nature around us we find only invariable and resistless sequences similar to the sequence of sin and shame and degradation already noticed in the world within. There is no word in the material world about pardon for the guilty, or about liberation for the captive. It is true that the plentiful fruits of the earth seem to declare that the Creator is good. But apparently the blessings of nature are only for those who obey its laws. Indeed the invariable sequences and the resistless forces of nature rather increase the terrors of the condemnation within. For they suggest that it is armed with irresistible power and knows nothing of mercy.

As yet we have found no confirmation of the salvation proclaimed in the New Testament. For this we must look in another direction. We shall not look in vain.

SECTION IV.

CHRISTIANITY COMPARED WITH OTHER RELIGIONS.

From the silent testimony of the material world we now turn to evidence afforded by the social life of our fellow-men. And, of some of the facts which will come before us in this field of research, we shall trace the development in the past history of the human race.

Of the social life of man, no feature is more conspicuous than Religion. Wherever there are buildings we see temples erected, and worship offered, to beings whom no human eye has ever seen. And all sorts of men believe that beyond death retribution awaits them for actions done in the present life. Moreover, the costliness of the gifts laid upon the altars of the gods, and the efforts, often painful and prolonged, to obtain their favour and to win happiness after death, reveal the worshippers' firm faith that there are intelligent beings greater than themselves and a life beyond the grave, and that man s wellbeing here and hereafter depends upon the smile or frown of these unseen powers.

Religion, in its various forms, is a note of distinction between men and brutes. Of these last, the entire action can be easily explained by the needs and desires of their bodily life. They live "according to the flesh," and by so doing attain the highest wellbeing possible to them. But for man so to live is felt to be shameful degradation; and tends to his destruction. The religions of mankind are an effort, often weak and sometimes terribly perverted, to rise to something better than the life of animals. And they reveal man's consciousness of things greater and better than those which he can see and touch.

The religions of men present, at first sight, a bewildering variety. But closer inspection detects many elements common to all. In spite of an admixture in many cases of elements immoral in their tendency, all religions pay honour to the supreme majesty of the Moral Law, and assert Moral Retribution. Indeed, this homage to an authority to which all are compelled to bow gives to the various forms of religion their first claim to the respect of men. And, as we have already seen, all religions must be judged at the bar of the Moral Law. Almost all religions assert that beyond and above the material world is an unseen Creator and Father and Moral Governor of all men. With this Supreme Lord are often associated other lower yet superhuman beings who for good or ill influence the action and the destiny of men. Touching these lower personalities religious opinions vary greatly. But nearly all religions acknowledge a Supreme Lord, and all pay homage to the Moral Law.

Among these many and various beliefs, one religion occupies a position of unique superiority. Of this pre-eminence two elements have already been noticed. The teaching and especially the character of Jesus appeal to our moral sense, to the tribunal within at whose bar all religions must be judged, with an authority possessed by no moral teaching independent of Christianity. And He differs from all other teachers in that He proclaims to all who believe His word forgiveness of past sins, and promises to breathe into them, by His own presence in their hearts, a disposition to love the right and the good and a moral power to do it. Other conspicuous elements of superiority, of an altogether different kind, now demand attention.

In all forms of material good, and especially in progress sustained during long centuries, all Christian nations stand immeasurably above all others.

In spite of their many wars, the Christian nations of Europe form in a very real sense a political brotherhood. In this brotherhood there reigns, as in a family, in spite of great difference of political power, a recognition of equality. The rights of the weakest are respected; and the power of the strongest is limited. Of that brotherhood, through sheer incapacity, no non-Christian nation is a member. No Christian nation treats, or can treat, with Turkey as on equal terms. No Christian nation would tolerate the interference with its internal administration to which again and again Turkey has submitted. Nor would any Christian nation try to impose on another such interference. Even the vast population of China, equal probably to that of the six great powers of Europe combined, does not make that empire equal in political influence to any one of these. As compared with Christian nations, every non-Christian nation stands on a definitely lower level.

Still more conspicuous is the difference in military power. No army has the slightest hope of victory in the field unless armed with the weapons and directed by the strategy of Christian nations. Even the once conquering

Turk must remodel his army in Christian fashion and seek for Christian leaders. And even then his prospects of permanent victory are not great. The sword has passed into the hands of those nations which recognise the unique majesty of the lowly Nazarene.

Military power must be counted, even by lovers of peace, an element of material good. For it guards our homes, makes impossible the overthrow of civilisation by barbarism, and gives to us a security unknown in earlier days.

Art also owns the supremacy of Christ. Non-Christian nations contribute nothing to our galleries of sculpture and painting, or to the world's treasury of music. Science bears similar testimony. The wonderful progress during the present century in our knowledge of the material world lifeless and living has been confined to professedly Christian peoples. This is acknowledged, half-unconsciously, by the foremost non-Christian nations who, waking up from long sleep, turn for instruction to European teachers. Literature also belongs to nations professedly Christian. Every year our libraries receive, in increasing number, foreign books and translations of such. But with the exception of ancient books translated by Europeans, these foreign works are almost all from Christian nations. In short, of every form of culture as of every kind of power, a practical monopoly is possessed by the nations which acknowledge the supremacy of Christ.

This monopoly becomes the more remarkable when we remember that art, science, and culture, and political and military power, did not owe their origin to Christianity but were born and attained considerable development long before Christ began to teach and far away from the nation which was waiting for His appearance. The ancient heathen world presents many examples of splendid military skill. The fabric of modern law rests upon the basis of Roman law. The artists of our day draw inspiration still from careful study of the art of ancient Greece. In the same race, or possibly in races which attained their prime even earlier than Greece, science had its beginning. And the masterpieces of ancient Greece are to-day the noblest schools of literary culture.

But when Christ was born, the culture of Greece had long passed its prime, and the power of Rome bore already seeds of decay. That decay was not arrested by the conversion of the Roman Empire to Christianity. The empire, containing within itself almost all the followers of Christ, trembled again and again before the onslaught of barbarian and heathen invaders. And it seemed as though beneath their rough might both civilisation and Christianity would be buried. On another side, the sword of Islam swept for a time all obstacles from its path, subdued some of the fairest lands of Christendom, and in these lands almost blotted out the Christian name. Even so lately as the sixteenth century, the nations of Europe trembled at the advance of the Turk. Later still, in A.D. 1683, a Turkish army besieged Vienna. And in architecture, science, and literature, at one time the followers of Mohammed held a high place.

All this has completely passed away. Christ and the early Christian teachers claimed no political power, and held out to their followers no hopes of such power. They said little or nothing about intellectual culture. But such was the influence of their teaching that within three centuries of the death of Christ the greatest ruler in the world thought fit to acknowledge the supreme royalty of Christ. The barbarian invaders accepted the religion, and with it the civilisation, of the empire they trampled under foot. The arm which once wielded the sword of Islam has been utterly paralysed. And whatever political power remains to the followers of Mohammed seems ready to pass away. Imperceptibly and silently, Christ has laid His hand upon every form of material good, and has given it to the nations which acknowledge His sway.

Very conspicuous is the sustained progress of Christian nations, in contrast to the stagnation or decadence of all others. In sustained progress, modern history presents a marked contrast to the history of the ancient world. Long before Christ came, there were mighty empires. But they had, so far as we can trace them, little permanence. Egypt and Assyria when first they came into the clear light of history were already in decay. The splendid empire of Nebuchadnezzar rose, culminated, and fell, within the lifetime of the prophet Daniel. The Persian empire soon became effete. The military prowess, the art, the literature, of Greece began to fade almost as soon as they had reached their bloom. The solid empire of Rome was erected on the crushed liberties of the Roman people. But for a thousand years the history of the nations of Christendom has been a history of progress. There have been times of apparent retrogression. But it has been only the momentary retreat of the incoming tide. Some Christian nations have lagged behind others. But it has been the joy of this generation to witness the advance of even the most backward.

As yet nothing has been said about progress in the sense of right, in mutual kindness, and in all that makes up the higher life of man. This kind of progress is less conspicuous than the material advance just mentioned. But it is far more important. When Christ was born, the world was sinking hopelessly, in spite of considerable culture, into deeper and deeper moral corruption. To-day, with all the many blemishes of modern life, there is in all Christian nations real moral improvement, apparent in the habits of society, in a purer public opinion, and in more earnest effort to help the weak and the unfortunate. In all other countries there is moral stagnation, except so far as they are influenced by Christian nations.

This monopoly of sustained progress by the professedly Christian nations is the most remarkable feature of human life and of human history. From the earliest dawn of history to the present day there has been general progress in every form of material and moral good. Before Christ came that progress was scattered over many widely-separated nations. It was also fitful; and its forms were transient. In His day, its force seemed to be spent: and apparently universal and hopeless decay had set in. But now a new element comes silently on the scene. Amid the ruins of the ancient civilisation a new civilisation, a new morality, and a new hope begin to develop. A new progress, slow but sure, is soon detected. The progress is maintained. In every department of human excellence we note advance. Out of the chaos of the ancient world rises the solid structure of modern society. And, strangest of all, this wonderful progress in everything that pertains to human welfare is found only in those nations which recognise the supreme authority of an obscure and apparently untrained Teacher who was laid in the grave before He had reached the prime of life. It is not too much to say that to-day every Christian nation is rising in material and moral good; and that no non-Christian nation is rising mentally or morally except by contact with Christian nations. This remarkable phenomenon demands explanation.

It is right to admit that in all Christian countries thousands set at nought and trample under foot the express commands of Christ, that not a few utterly neglect all the ordinances of religion, and that some deny even the existence of God. But all this by no means proves that these persons are not benefited by the Christianity they neglect or reject. For we are often greatly, though unconsciously, affected by influences which we resolutely resist. In Christian countries Christian influences are everywhere and always operating. The mass of the people recognise Jesus of Nazareth as incomparably the greatest Teacher the world has ever known. His words are more or less familiar to them. To Him they turn in their better moments. And by His teaching, directly or indirectly, their moral sense is raised and strengthened. Moreover, in all professedly Christian lands the number of sincere servants of Christ is far larger than at first sight appears. Wickedness is conspicuous: goodness delights to hide itself from the gaze of others. But though hidden, like leaven, the influence of genuine Christians for good permeates the entire community.

It is also right to admit that many of the most conspicuous leaders in natural science during the last fifty years have themselves rejected the distinctive features of Christianity. Yet most of them pay homage to Christ as the greatest moral Teacher of any age or nation. They thus bear reluctant witness to the moral authority of One whose personal claims they reject as absurd. And we must not forget that these anti-Christian teachers have themselves been trained in a moral and intellectual atmosphere formed by many centuries of Christian influences. Outside of Christendom we find to-day and for many centuries past no progress even in natural science. Moreover, the very recent date of this anti-Christian teaching forbids us to base any argument upon it. Time is needed to test its effect upon the highest interests of men. Certainly, no inference drawn from a small fragment of the race during one or two generations can have any force against an induction based upon the present state of every nation in the world, and upon the past history of these nations during the many centuries illumined by the light of history. Whether the moral teaching and influence of those who reject Christianity will benefit or injure our race remains to be seen. As yet, such men have done very little directly to lessen human sorrow or to develop the higher side of human life.

The unique position of Christianity among the nations is not made less remarkable, although its influence for good is lessened, by the many divisions of the followers of Christ. For these divisions do but slightly veil a wonderful underlying unity. All Christians agree to assert that Jesus of Nazareth is incomparably the Greatest Moral Teacher that has ever lived. And, with exceptions too few to mention, they all agree in the remarkable belief that the Crucified One is in a unique and sublime sense the Eternal Son of God and the Creator of the universe; that in order to save man He became Man; that in order to remove a barrier between God and man caused by man's sin He willingly submitted to die; that He rose from the dead; and that He will return in splendour to raise the dead, to judge all men, and to set up an Eternal Kingdom. That these remarkable doctrines are held firmly and are greatly prized by almost all religious men in all the foremost nations of the world, and that these nations hold the position already described, are facts which ought to arrest attention and which certainly demand explanation.

Of the pre-eminence of the Christian nations, no explanation can be found except in their Christianity. For this is the only element they have in common and in distinction from other nations. Their position in the world cannot be attributed to race. For the Hindus and the Persians are, as their languages prove, kinsmen of the European nations. From the thirsty lands beyond the Caspian two savage hordes, branches of the same Turanian race, poured at different times into Europe. The one came along the Northern, the other along the Southern shores of the Black Sea. In their barbarity there was little or nothing to choose. But the one horde accepted Christianity. The other embraced Islam. And to-day the descendants of the one, the Hungarians, march in the front rank of the nations of the world: the Turkish race, with few regrets, is decaying and dying before our eyes. The Finns also do not belong to the great Indo-Germanic race. And certainly their climate is barbarous. But they are Christians. And they hold their rightful and recognised place in the family of Christian nations. In the Turkish Empire are many Christians who for ages have groaned under terrible tyranny. Naturally, they have felt the debasing influence of bondage. But by the admission of the Turks themselves, given sometimes consciously, sometimes unconsciously, they are by far the most hopeful and progressive element of the empire. Japan has had a wonderful awakening. But it seems to have been caused by contact with Christian nations. And to these certainly Japan is now turning for help along the newly-entered path of progress.

Look where we will, a great fact as wide as the world arrests our attention. Wherever there is Christianity, we see superiority and growth: wherever Christianity is not, we see inferiority and stagnation. So far-reaching is the correspondence that it cannot be accidental. Either Christianity raises those who receive it; or it commends itself to all rising nations. And each of these suppositions implies unique excellence. And both are in part true. That the former supposition is correct, the story of the nations proves. For the more part, in the darkness of barbarism they accepted the Gospel: and they then rose slowly into new light and life. A survey of the present state and past history of our race leaves no room for doubt that Christianity is the source of the pre-eminence of the foremost nations. And, if so, it is the mightiest power for good which the world has ever known. For the secret of its power, we must seek.

In our search for an explanation of the facts now before us, we turn to the past history of our race. Our special aim is to find the steps by which the unique religion mounted to its place of power.

Christianity arose suddenly out of an obscure nation and out of a national religion.

In the ancient world, the Jewish race occupies a unique place. Its Sacred Books never stoop to favour or tolerate idolatry. They speak ever of One Personal God, the Creator of the world; and reveal an actual intercourse with Him and confidence in Him which is unique in ancient literature. Not less conspicuous is the joyful expectation, here and there expressed, of world-wide and glorious blessings to come. The same books contain an intelligible account of the beginning of the world; and a national history without parallel for its completeness. In its assured knowledge of God the Jewish nation stood alone, at the time of Christ, among the nations of the world.

Yet, in spite of its immense superiority, the religion of the Jews had made little mark on the religious thought and life of the nations around. Doubtless on the minds of not a few the loftier conceptions of God embodied in the Jewish Scriptures and read in the synagogues of the Dispersion had produced a deep impression. In this way the scattered Jews were forerunners of the Gospel. But on the nations around the influence of the Jewish religion was but slight. And, at the birth of Christ, the race itself, like all others around, seemed to have passed its prime. It cherished memories of political power and material prosperity in days long gone by. But national independence was irrevocably lost. The long line of prophets and teachers had ceased. In the sacred land disorder prevailed. Nothing remained to Israel in the wide-spread and deepening gloom but the hope of a coming Deliverer.

Unexpectedly, in the first century, the scene was entirely changed. The little rill of spiritual life which for many centuries had trickled unobserved among the nations suddenly spread into a great river and overspread the mightiest empire of the world, then passed its vast boundaries, and is now spreading to the ends of the earth. Or, more correctly, within the little rill arose another rill which became a river, and then widened into an ocean; while the original rill continued its old course narrower and poorer for the river to which it had given birth.

The new movement was a spiritual revolution within the Jewish nation. While reasserting emphatically the best elements of the teaching of the Old Testament, the early Christian teachers proclaimed, as we shall see, and developed to their logical consequences, doctrines found in the ancient writings only in germ. And these new doctrines became the distinctive beliefs of the communities they founded.

Thus arose the Christian Church. Within fifty years of the death of Christ Christian communities were found throughout the Roman Empire. Within three hundred years, the Emperor Constantine sought admission within its pale. An attempt by the Emperor Julian to revive the ancient faiths only proved that they were beyond revival. Meanwhile the Church lived on, strangely corrupted by the corruptions around, but always containing the germs of new life. Christianity was accepted by the barbarian conquerors of Rome, and restrained the fury which otherwise would have destroyed the civilisation of the ancient world. By doing this, it rendered to the whole human race a service which can never be estimated.

Meanwhile in Arabia arose a new teacher, proclaiming the unity and spirituality of God, retribution beyond the grave, and certain rude outlines of morality. This teaching commended itself to the moral sense of the children of the desert. We need not wonder that they accepted Mohammed as a teacher sent from God. Spiritual success gave to him political and military power: and with the sword his followers went forth to conquer. In most directions their onslaught was irresistible. Fortunately it was arrested by the bulwarks of Constantinople. A strange empire was founded. Under its wing flourished architecture, science, and philosophy. But the rising tide soon reached its height. The sword of Islam lost its power. Its culture did not long survive. To-day, in every form of human power and progress the followers of Mohammed are hopelessly in the rear of the Christian nations. For many centuries, sustained progress has been found only in those nations which recognise the carpenter of Nazareth as incomparably the greatest of men.

An apparent exception to the above statement may be found in the Jewish nationality as now existing. In Christian countries the Jews have, without giving up their own religion, appropriated the culture and shared the material prosperity of those among whom they live. That under such circumstances they have retained their religion, proves its superiority to other non-Christian religions. They are equal to their Christian neighbours in intelligence, morality, and beneficence. And we need not wonder if in

Mohammedan and heathen countries their purer faith raises them above surrounding races. But I do not know that this superiority is universal or great. The effect of the Jewish faith on the life of an independent nation, we have no opportunity of measuring. Hitherto Judaism has been only a thread interwoven among other threads. We therefore cannot estimate its strength to sustain the weight of independent political life and to raise a people into progressive material and moral wellbeing. The contrast between the obscure religion of ancient Israel, possessing the highest moral teaching yet influencing only slightly and almost imperceptibly the nations around, and the transforming and wide-spread effect of the teaching of Christ, is an element of the case before us specially demanding explanation.

Looking now at all these facts, at the story of the ancient nations, at the state of the world when Christ was born, at its subsequent history, at the state of the various nations of the world to-day, it is impossible to deny that Christianity has rescued our race from the anarchy and ruin into which at the Christian Era it was rapidly falling. Eliminate Christianity from the history of the first thousand years of our era, and conceive the result. Nothing remains except the burial of civilisation under the tread of barbarous invaders; as seems to have been the case in pre-historic America. And with the effect of Christianity in the past agrees the fact that to-day it is coextensive with political and military power, and culture, and progress. In view of all this, it is not too much to say that Christianity has saved the world. When Christ was born, the world was helplessly and hopelessly sinking.

For many long centuries it has been rising. And for this great change, no cause can be found except the influence of Christ and His followers. Certainly, this change is the greatest fact of human history. No philosophy of history or of social life is worthy of consideration unless it do something to account for this remarkable phenomenon. We must seek for a power sufficient to produce results so far-reaching and so vast.

SECTION V.

CHRIST, AND THE CHRISTIAN DOCUMENTS.

THE influence of Christianity must be attributed to Christ. For all Christian literature of every age and nation points to Him as the unique source of every blessing. To Him bows every act, word, thought, of the Christian life. And the dignity of their Master was, as we shall soon see, a great part of the teaching of His early followers. The entire history of the world affords no example of personal influence and of devotion to, and confidence in, a person which can for a moment be compared to the influence exerted by, and the devotion paid to, Jesus of Nazareth. This influence reveals a unique Personality. To Him therefore we must look as the Author of the moral impulse which, beginning in the first century and operating continuously till our own day, has changed the entire course of human history and has saved the world from ruin.

It will be remembered that already the moral teaching attributed in the New Testament to Christ and the example of Christ have commanded the profound homage of whatever in us is noblest and best, that the personal influence of Christ as there portrayed has been to thousands the strongest motive to virtue they have ever known, and that the salvation recorded as offered by Christ commended itself to us as a complete supply of our moral and spiritual need. We have now learned that, as matter of historic fact, the Great Teacher there portrayed is the Author of a moral and spiritual impulse which has saved the world.

Similarly, the Buddhist and Mohammedan movements must be attributed to the men whose names they bear. Indeed these three great religions, each claiming a personal Founder, are worthy of careful comparison, in the character of their founders, in their moral and theological teaching, in their past influence upon the world, and in the present condition of their adherents.

We therefore ask eagerly, Who was Jesus, what did He teach and do, what was the secret of His incomparable personal influence and of the wonderful effect of that influence upon the world?

Our question is historic. It pertains to alleged matters of fact. And we must seek for an answer by strictly historical methods, as we should about any other matter which had not come under our own observation. We must collect all available witnesses, examine their credentials, listen to their testimony, and thus endeavour to reach a reliable judgment.

Inasmuch as we are dealing now with a matter separated from us by long centuries, our only witnesses at this stage of our inquiry are written documents.

We have nothing from the pen of Christ. But several letters have come down to us professing to have been written by the most conspicuous of His followers, the earliest Apostle who preached the Gospel in Europe.

With these are associated other extant letters and documents which in the latter part of the second century were accepted throughout the Roman Empire as written by immediate disciples of Christ or by their later contemporaries.

The first five books of the New Testament are anonymous. For the names commonly attached to the four Gospels, although found in our earliest copies, are doubtless of later date and do but embody a very ancient tradition. We therefore pass over these books for the moment, in favour of thirteen letters which bear the name of the Apostle Paul and thus make a definite claim touching their authorship. All these were accepted throughout the Roman Empire with perfect confidence as genuine works of the great Apostle. The first four epistles have been accepted in all ages and countries by all scholars, with exceptions too few and unimportant to mention, as undoubtedly written by Paul. How solid is the foundation on which rests this unanimous conviction, I have at considerable length endeavoured to show in my commentaries on these epistles.[1] In another volume I hope soon to show that we may with confidence accept as genuine the Epistles to the Ephesians, Philippians, and Colossians. But these, though confirming it, are not needful for my present argument. It rests securely upon the four epistles acknowledged to be genuine by many who reject as untrue, and even absurd, the doctrines so firmly held by their illustrious writer.

That these letters as presented to us in the Revised Version are a correct reproduction of the words actually

---

[1] See especially *Corinthians*, p. 499.

written by St. Paul, I have also, in the volumes referred to, endeavoured to show.

These epistles afford us, in our present research, immense help. For they span over at once the great interval which separates us from the days of Christ, and place us in the presence of one of His contemporaries. In them we see reflected the impression made by Christ upon the mind of one of the most intelligent of His immediate followers. This reflection is an important step towards understanding the actual teaching and claims of Christ.

In these letters we also find portrayed unmistakeably on every page the mental and moral character of the writer. We notice at once his calm and balanced judgment, looking always at both sides of a question, and his constant habit of tracing details to broad principles; his moral earnestness, and his unselfish and thoughtful care for others; his deep patriotism combined with wide human sympathy and complete freedom from both Jewish and anti-Jewish prejudices; his reverence for the Ancient Law and his earnest assertion that we are no longer under law but under grace.[1] It is no small gain that we are able to derive our first impressions of the historic Christ from a witness so exalted and so trustworthy.

We must now endeavour to reproduce, in scanty outline, St. Paul's conception of the Gospel and of Christ.

For such reproduction, the Epistle to the Romans is our best authority. For, unlike the other three epistles, which were written about personal matters to Churches known

[1] See further in my *Romans*, p. 381, *Corinthians*, pp. 490-93.

personally to Paul, this epistle, written to men whom he had never seen, and having apparently no special occasion, sets forth in systematic order the Gospel as Paul understood it.

In ch. i. 1–7 we have a formal introduction; in vers. 8–15, sundry personal matters. In vers. 16, 17, the writer gives a compact description of the Gospel he desires to preach at Rome. It is a power of God for salvation to all who believe; because in it is revealed a righteousness of God through faith and for faith. After a digression occupying ch. i. 18–iii. 20 and proving that all men everywhere need such a gospel, Paul repeats in ch. iii. 21, 22 his description of it in almost identical terms. Ver. 23 recapitulates his proof that all men need the Gospel. In vers. 24, 26 the verb *justify* (rendered *being justified* and *justifier*) is evidently equivalent to the abstract substantive *righteousness*, and recapitulates the statement in vers. 21, 22. The latter word denotes the state of one who is righteous; the former, the act of making righteous. In vers. 28 and 30 we have the same verb again, and a double repetition of Paul's main assertion. He declares that "by faith a man is justified," and that "God will justify the circumcision by faith and the uncircumcision through faith." This assertion, so emphatically repeated, is supported in ch. iv. by a careful exposition of Abraham's faith, which is held up in ver. 24 as a pattern to the men of Paul's own day. The same doctrine meets us again in ch. ix. 30–x. 13. It is also very conspicuous in almost the same terms in Gal. ii. 16, iii. 2–14. From all this we infer with confidence that, as matter of historic fact, Paul taught that they who believe are justified; and that this doctrine was a conspicuous element of the Gospel he preached.

This inference, already secure, receives remarkable confirmation from an altogether independent witness. The anonymous document known as *The Acts of the Apostles* was accepted among Christians throughout the Roman Empire in the latter part of the second century without a shadow of doubt or mention of any other author as written by Luke, a companion and friend of Paul. This proves its great antiquity. And its complete independence is proved by the absence in it of any reference to the epistles of Paul. This new witness, in ch. xiii. 39, represents the Apostle Paul as saying in an address at Antioch in Pisidia that in Christ "everyone that believeth is justified from all things" from which none "could be justified in the Law of Moses." This coincidence is the more remarkable because no other contemporary speaks of justification through faith. Taken in connexion with his epistles, it is plain proof that this doctrine was actually taught by the great Apostle.

We now ask, What is the meaning of the words which we have traced to his pen and to his lips? An answer must be sought in the common use of these words in his day and in the circles in which he moved.

The Greek word rendered *justify* in the New Testament is a constant equivalent for a Hebrew word found in two closely related forms. One of these is found in Job xxxii. 2, "Job justified himself rather than God;" and in ch. xxxiii. 32, "If thou hast anything to say, answer me: Speak, for I desire to justify thee." In a similar sense it is found also in Jer. iii. 11, Ezek. xvi. 51, 52; but does not occur elsewhere. The other Hebrew form is a technical term for a judge's sentence in a man's favour. So Deut. xxv. 1: "If there be a controversy between men, and they come to judgment, and the judges judge them: then they shall justify the righteous and condemn the wicked." And Prov. xvii. 15: "He that justifieth the wicked, and he that condemneth the righteous, both of them alike are an abomination to the Lord." Also in 1 Kings viii. 32: "Hear Thou in heaven, and do, and judge thy servants, condemning the wicked, to bring his way upon his own head; and justifying the righteous, to give him according to his righteousness." Similar use of the same word in Isa. v. 23, 2 Chron. vi. 23, Exod. xxiii. 7, Isa. l. 8. These passages fix the meaning of the word *justify*. It cannot denote the act of making a person actually righteous. To justify the wicked, in this sense, could not be an abomination to the Lord. The word evidently means to reckon or declare a person righteous, or to treat him as such. In the same sense it is found in the Gospels. From "her children" or "her works," as we read in Matt. xi. 19, Luke vii. 35, has gone forth a declaration that wisdom is in the right. The men mentioned in Luke x. 29, xvi. 15, declared themselves righteous, seeking to make themselves such in the subjective view of others, or perhaps even of themselves. So in Luke vii. 29 Christ speaks of some who "justified God." By accepting the Baptism of John they proclaimed that God was right in His severe words to them through the lips of the strange preacher. Matt. xii. 37 refers expressly, as does Rom. ii. 13, to a favourable sentence of God at the Great Assize. Throughout the Greek Bible, the word either has indisputably, or will easily admit, this sense. And this must have been the meaning intended by Paul in the passages quoted above.

An important confirmation of this meaning is found in Rom. iv. 5, 6, where the statement that faith in Him who justifies the ungodly is reckoned for rightuousness is supported by a quotation from the Psalms: " Blessed are they whose iniquities are forgiven, and whose sins are covered. Blessed is the man to whom the Lord will not reckon sin." Inasmuch as all men are sinners, evangelical justification is practically pardon. So in Acts xiii. 39, already quoted, the declaration that all believers are justified is prefaced by an assertion that through Christ " is preached forgiveness of sins." [1]

The Apostle Paul's teaching about faith as the means of justification is equally clear. The justified are said in Rom. iv. 12 to walk in the steps of the faith of their father Abraham. Now Abraham's faith was belief of a definite promise made to him by God: "according to that which was spoken, So shall thy seed be." And the announcement that God justifies all who believe is practically a promise to them of eternal life. In other words, justifying faith is a personal assurance resting upon the promise of God that God will give eternal life to each one who accepts that promise, and therefore to the assured one himself.

We have now learnt that, as matter of history, Paul taught that God receives into His favour all those who believe the good news of pardon through faith; and that this teaching was a chief element of the Gospel he preached.

---

[1] Compare Eph. i. 7 ; Col. i. 14, ii. 13.

This Gospel, as he tells us in Gal. i. 11, 12, Paul received from Christ. And his epistles reveal everywhere his complete confidence that it came from the lips of the Great Master.

We now ask, Has Paul correctly understood, in the matter before us, the teaching of Christ, or is his conception of the Gospel coloured and distorted by his own subjectivity? To answer this question, we must seek other and independent testimony.

The four Gospels contain short accounts of the life and teaching and death of Christ. The so-called First Epistle of John is a sort of comment on the words attributed to Christ in the Fourth Gospel. Both documents are undoubtedly from the same pen. They were accepted before the close of the second century in widely separated parts of the empire without any doubt as written by a specially beloved disciple and apostle of Christ. This universal reception proves at once that they were written not much later than the beginning of the century. And we find very much internal evidence that they were actually written by the Apostle John.[1] Together these two documents embody a marked type of teaching, one differing very much in phraseology and modes of thought from the teaching of Paul. In them we have an independent and very early witness about the Gospel. Comparison of the two types of doctrine will enable us to eliminate from each the personal element, and to reach the actual teaching of Christ.

We miss at once the distinctive phraseology of Paul. The words *justify* and *justification* never occur. The sub-

---

[1] See Westcott's *Introduction to the Gospel of John* in *The Speaker's Commentary*.

stantive *faith* is found only in 1 John v. 4. And not only the outward forms but the modes of thought are changed. But underneath this outward dissimilarity we find substantial agreement.

In John iii. 16 Christ is represented as saying that God gave His Son in order that every one who believes in Him may not perish but may have eternal life; and as going on to say in ver. 18 that whoever believes in Him is not judged. Several times we are told that every one who believes in Christ has already eternal life: so ch. iii. 36, v. 24, vi. 35, 47, xi. 25. The believer "has passed out of death into life:" ch. v. 24. This teaching is one of the most conspicuous features of the Fourth Gospel. In the Epistle we are told (ch. i. 7) that God "is faithful and just to forgive us our sins:" and in ch. ii. 12 the writer says to his readers, "I write to you, little children, because your sins are forgiven you." In short, in spite of the totally dissimilar phraseology, revealing the complete independence of the documents, the doctrines which we have proved to have been taught by Paul are in the Fourth Gospel expressly attributed to Christ.

The First Gospel presents another type of teaching quite different, as has been most eagerly pointed out by many scholars, from both the types we have already examined. And very closely associated with it is the Epistle of James. In these documents we have a third independent witness.

As His words are recorded in Matt. vi. 14, ix. 2-6, xii. 31, 32, Christ promises or proclaims forgiveness of sins. In ch. xxvi. 28, He declares in circumstances the most solemn, "This is My blood of the Covenant, which is shed for forgiveness of sins." Similar testimony is borne in Mark ii. 5 – 10, iii. 28, xi. 25; Luke v. 20 – 24, vii. 47–49, xi. 4.

In the first three Gospels, and especially in the first of the three, forgiveness of sins is not connected with faith in the conspicuous way in which faith and eternal life are linked together in the Fourth Gospel. But we notice that faith is a constant condition of blessing from God. Among other passages I may quote Matt. ix. 22, "Be of good cheer, daughter: thy faith hath saved thee." And in ver. 29 of the same chapter, to two blind men asking for help Christ is recorded to have said, "According to your faith be it done to you."

Put together now the evidence of these various witnesses, add to them the evidence afforded by some other independent documents contained in the New Testament, and test the whole by the principles on which we estimate alleged matters of fact which have not come under our own observation. The only way in which we can explain the similarity amid so great diversity is by admitting that the element common to these various witnesses was derived from a common source. And that source can only be the actual teaching of Christ. In other words, we are sure, as matter of historic fact, that He taught that God receives into His favour all who believe the good news announced by Christ. This result, obtained by the ordinary methods of historical criticism, abides firm, whatever we may think about the authority of Holy Scripture or of Christ. It is a definite gain in our present inquiry.

It is equally certain that Christ taught much more than the forgiveness of sins.

The Apostle Paul guards from abuse his doctrine of Justification through Faith by asserting plainly and repeatedly that God frowns upon all sin. After asserting and defending his great doctrine earnestly and effectively, he goes on to say in Gal. v. 21, after a list of sins, "Touching which things I say beforehand, as I have already before said, that they who do such things will not inherit the kingdom of God." So in 1 Cor. vi. 9: "Be not deceived; neither fornicators, nor idolaters, . . . will inherit the kingdom of God." Throughout his epistles we have other similar assertions. So in 1 John iii. 7: "He that doeth righteousness is righteous, according as He is righteous. He that doeth sin is of the devil. . . . In this are manifest the children of God and the children of the devil." In John v. 28, 29, Christ is recorded as teaching: "An hour cometh in which all that are in the graves will hear His voice and will go forth; they that have done the good things, for resurrection of life, and they that have done the bad things, for resurrection of judgment."

The above type of teaching, common throughout the New Testament, is specially conspicuous in the First Gospel. It guards from abuse the doctrine of forgiveness through faith by making faith impossible except to those who earnestly purpose to forsake all sin. For we cannot believe that we are in the way of life while walking along a path which He who promises life declares to lead to death, especially when the threatenings of Christ are re-echoed by the thunder of the Supreme Judge within. These re-echoed threatenings close every door of hope except the strait gate of repentance.

Another doctrine as remarkable as Justification through

Faith is equally conspicuous throughout the Epistles of Paul. After announcing righteousness through faith in Rom. iii. 21, 22, the Apostle goes on to say in vers. 24–26 that God set forth Christ to be a propitiation "in His blood;" and that God did this in order to be "Himself just and a justifier of him that hath faith in Jesus." This implies that apart from the death of Christ the justification even of believers would have been inconsistent with the justice of God. And, if so, it would have been impossible: for God cannot be unjust. Therefore, had He not died, we must; and Paul may rightly speak in ver. 24 and elsewhere of Him as our ransom price. The same teaching is implied in the frequent phrase "died for our sins" in 1 Cor. xv. 3 and elsewhere.

From this doctrine the Apostle draws in Rom. v. legitimate and important inferences. And in so doing he recapitulates the doctrine in vers. 6, 8, 9, 10 in the phrases, "Christ died for ungodly ones," "died for us," and says that we were "justified in His blood," and "reconciled to God through the death of His Son." In Rom. vii. 4, in a totally different argument he again sums up the same doctrine by saying that, just as a married woman is, by the death of her husband, made free from the legal obligation which forbad her remarriage, so we "have been put to death to the Law by the body of Christ." He can only mean that the death of the body of Christ upon the cross has removed a legal hindrance to our union with Christ. Compare also Gal. iii. 13, 14: "Christ hath redeemed us from the curse of the Law, having been made a curse on our behalf: for it is written, Cursed is every one that hangeth on a tree . . . that we may receive the promise of the Spirit through faith." Hence (ch. vi. 14) the cross of Christ, a badge of his nation's degradation, the instrument of the cruel death of his adored Master, is to Paul an object of exultation. This he explains by adding that on that cross himself has been crucified to the world and the world to him. Similar thoughts permeate all his epistles. Evidently the doctrine before us had moulded the entire thought of the great Apostle.

Naturally this doctrine is less prominent in the discourses spoken by Christ before His death than in letters written after it. But the remarkable words of Christ recorded in John vi. 53-56, "Except ye eat the flesh and drink the blood of the Son of God, ye have no life in you," teach plainly that our life comes through His death. For nutriment derived from eating flesh is purchased at the cost of life. Of similar significance are the Evangelist's explanation in John xi. 51 of the foregoing prophecy of Caiaphas, "This said he, not of himself, but being high priest of that year he prophesied that Jesus would die for the nation, and not for the nation only but in order that the scattered children of God may be gathered together;" and the words recorded in John xii. 24, "Except a grain of wheat fall into the ground and die, it abideth alone; but if it die, it beareth much fruit." The very strong language in 1 John i. 7, "The blood of Jesus, His Son, cleanseth us from all sin," is full of significance. The writer evidently means that, had not Christ's blood been shed, our impurity would not have been removed. And this is in complete harmony with the doctrine taught by Paul.

A most important coincidence with all this is found in

the account given in the Synoptist Gospels about the institution of the Lord's Supper. In Matt. xxvi. 28, Christ is represented as saying, "This is My blood of the Covenant, which is shed for many for remission of sins." Similar words are attributed to Him in Mark xiv. 24. In Luke xxii. 20, He is represented as saying, "This cup is the New Covenant in My blood, which is shed for you." These words teach, in a way which admits of no doubt, that the death of Christ is an essential element of that New Covenant, foretold in Jer. xxxi. 31, which promises forgiveness of sins. In other words, Paul's remarkable teaching that Christ gave Himself up to die in order to save men from the penalty of their sins is directly attributed to Christ, both in the Fourth Gospel, a document widely different in its modes of thought from the epistles of Paul, and in the three Synoptist Gospels, which differ equally from the writings of Paul and from those attributed to John.

The very important question how the death of Christ reconciles with the justice of God the justification of sinners, and thus removes the barrier to the favour of God erected by our sins, a question worthy of most careful and reverent study, lies beyond the scope of our present inquiry.

One more doctrine claims special attention. Paul teaches abundantly that to all who believe the Gospel God gives His Spirit to be in them the source of a new life, like the life of Christ; and to be in them the moral strength of Christ bursting and destroying the inward fetter of sin, and the wisdom of God guiding them along a path of safety into an ever-deepening knowledge of God as their Father in heaven. In Rom. viii. 2, the Apostle joyfully declares, "the Spirit of life in Christ Jesus hath made me free from the law of sin and of death." The sons of God (ver. 14) "are led by the Spirit of God." And in the Spirit they "cry Abba, Father." His presence in them makes their bodies to be the "temple of God:" 1 Cor. iii. 16, vi. 19. Of such teaching, the epistles of Paul are full.

Similarly, in John iii. 5, Christ declares to Nicodemus that only they who are "born of the Spirit" can enter into the kingdom of God. In ch. vii. 38, He uses language which the Evangelist explains by saying, "This spake He about the Spirit which they that believed on Him were to receive." The promise of the Spirit is a conspicuous element of Christ's discourse on the night of His betrayal: so John xiv. 16, 17, 26, xv. 26, xvi. 7, 8, 13, 14.

In close harmony with this teaching the Baptist foretold, as recorded in Matt. iii. 11, that Christ would baptize with the Holy Spirit. In ch. x. 20, Christ promises that when His disciples are brought before judges the Spirit of their Father shall speak in them. In Luke xi. 13 we have a universal promise: "How much more shall your Father in heaven give the Holy Spirit to those who ask Him."

' Further confirmation of the same teaching is very conspicuous throughout the Book of Acts. From the Day of Pentecost onwards, the presence of the Spirit in those who believe is a conspicuous feature of the Apostolic Churches. An Apostle could say (Acts v. 32) in the highest court of the Jews, "We are witnesses of these things, and so is the

Holy Spirit whom God hath given to those who believe Him."

The results just attained are of the highest importance. We have examined documents of which some were undoubtedly written by one of the most conspicuous of the early followers of Christ, and the others were in the latter part of the second century accepted with complete confidence as written either by Apostles or by their immediate associates. The manifest independence of these documents gives great significance to their doctrinal harmony. The only explanation of the whole case is that the doctrines held so firmly and yet expounded so variously were derived from the same source. And that source must have been the Great Teacher at whose feet sat all the Apostles.

We have now traced to the lips of Jesus of Nazareth certain great doctrines. He taught, as we have proved, that God receives into His favour all who believe the good news announced by Christ; that in order that He might justly smile on men God gave Christ to die; and that to those who believe He gives His Holy Spirit to be in them the animating principle of a new life.

It will be at once noticed that these three doctrines were before us in Section ii. We then listened to them, without scrutiny of their historic origin, simply as associated with moral teaching which appealed to us as the voice of an authority we could not gainsay and with a moral portrait which claimed at once our profound homage. In our darkness these doctrines gave us light. As we lay conscious of sin and afraid of punishment, the New Testament announced eternal life for all who believe. To men unable to break the fetters of moral bondage it promised deliverance. The completeness of the salvation offered was to us a strong presumption that it came from One who not only knew, but was able to supply, our deep need.

We have now learnt that, as matter of indisputable fact, this salvation was offered to men by the historic Author of the great moral impulse which changed the whole course of human history and rescued our race from the ruin into which in His day it was sinking. The historic effects of the teaching of Jesus are a further presumption that the doctrines before us are true.

But these presumptions do not quite satisfy us. The vastness of the issues at stake demand a still more solid foundation for our faith. Christ claims our belief as the condition of the blessings He offers. But an intelligent man cannot believe until he knows who it is that claims his confidence. Nay more. The Judge within forbids us to accept the voice of pardon until we have proof that it speaks with an authority equal to that which condemns us. With the profound reverence due to a great moral teacher we ask, Who is Jesus, and what right has He to loose the bonds which the eternal Law of Righteousness has forged? For this question, we now seek an answer.

It is at once evident, not so much from the passages quoted above as from the entire tenor of his epistles, that St. Paul accepted these doctrines with perfect confidence, that they silenced in him the condemnation of conscience and gave to him an assured hope of life and glory beyond the grave. We naturally inquire, How was it that the pupil of Gamaliel received the teaching of the Carpenter of Nazareth as, even in a matter of infinite importance, absolutely decisive? How was it that the moral sensitiveness of Paul, so conspicuous throughout his epistles, found rest, even in view of his previous deadly hostility to what he afterwards learnt to be the truth, in the assertions of so humble a teacher? Paul's firm belief of the Gospel reveals the deep impression made upon him by the personality of Christ. This impression, on the mind of Paul and of his contemporaries, we must now endeavour to reproduce. Our aim in so doing is to reach the actual teaching of Jesus touching Himself.

We notice, throughout his epistles, St. Paul's profound reverence for Christ as infinitely the greatest of men. He counts it highest honour to be a servant of Jesus Christ. In 2 Cor. ii. 14, he rejoices to be led as a captive in the train of so glorious a conqueror. The portrait of Christ reflected in the writings of Paul and in the four Gospels deserves now our careful study.

The Apostle speaks of Christ constantly as in a distinctive sense *the Son of God*. In Rom. viii. 32 (cp. ver. 3) he calls Him *the own Son* of God even in contrast to those on whose behalf God gave Him up to die. That this gift is appealed to as a proof of God's love to us, implies that Christ's relation to God is different in kind and nearer than ours. For there is a tacit comparison to a father who gives up his own son to die in order to save others. That Paul taught, as we have already seen, that God gave Christ to die in order to reconcile with His own justice the justification of believers, implies that Christ is sinless and equal in moral worth to the whole race. His comparison of Christ to Adam in Rom. v. 14–19 implies that, just as evidently Adam's relation to the race is unique, so also is that of Christ. In the great Day, when every man will stand powerless to be judged, Christ will sit as Judge. So 2 Cor. v. 10: "We all must needs appear before the judgment-seat of Christ." If, as we have good reason to believe, the Epistle to the Colossians is genuine, Paul teaches (Col. i. 16) that He who will be the Judge is also the Creator of the world. Indisputably Paul looked upon Christ as infinitely greater than man.

We turn now to the Gospels, which profess to give us Christ's testimony touching Himself. And we find equally conspicuous there, as claimed by Himself, the surpassing dignity given to Him by Paul. In John iii. 16, 18, Christ calls Himself *the only-begotten Son* of God, thus claiming a unique relation to God. He is the only *way* to God. So ch. xiv. 6: "No one cometh to the Father except through Me." His voice will call the dead to judgment: ch. v. 29. So ch. vi. 39, 44, 54. He made assertions about Himself which His enemies understood (ch. v. 18, x. 33) to mean equality with God. Yet His biographer gives no hint that they had wrongly interpreted His words. Nay more. Thomas accosts Him with the august title: "My Lord and my God." And Jesus accepts it as an expression of faith. The writer of the Fourth Gospel calmly asserts that Christ is *God*; and strengthens this assertion by saying that by His agency were made all things which have been made.

In the Synoptist Gospels, similar honour is paid to Christ. The title Son of God is given to Him by a voice from heaven in Matt. iii. 17, Mark i. 11, Luke iii. 22. The same title given to Him by Peter in Matt. xvi. 16 is said to be a revelation from God. Even as compared with the prophets of the Old Covenant, whom He describes as *servants*, Christ claims to be the Master's *Son*. So Matt. xxi. 37, Luke xx. 13, and especially Mark xii. 6, "He had one beloved Son." (Same comparison in Heb. iii. 6, where Moses is a "servant" and therefore "in the household" as a part of it, and Christ is a "son over the household.") This comparison is most significant. For all know the difference in the palace between the highest servant and the King's Son. This superiority above the greatest of His predecessors, Christ claims. In Matt. xiii. 41, xvi. 27, xxiv. 31, xxv. 34, 41; Mark xiii. 27, He announces that at the end of the world, from a throne of glory, He will pronounce judgment on all men.

The wide differences, both in phraseology and in modes of thought, already noted between the Epistles of Paul, the Fourth Gospel, and the Synoptists, give immense significance to the close agreement in their estimate of Christ. Each group of witnesses speaks of Him as, or quote Him as claiming to be, in a unique sense the Son of God and the future Judge of all men. These independent but closely agreeing testimonies, coming at least in part from contemporaries of Christ, can be explained only by admitting that He claimed these titles. This we may accept as an assured result of our study of the Christian documents.

It is worthy of note that Pliny in his letter to the Emperor Trajan speaks of the Christians as singing hymns to Christ as God. And the Christian literature of the first two centuries speaks ever in the same strain.

Paul's confident acceptance of the momentous teaching of Christ, and the wonderful effect of that teaching upon his thought and heart and life, are now in some measure explained by his equally confident belief that Jesus of

Nazareth is far greater than the greatest of men. We need not wonder that, in the presence of one whom he believed to be the Own Son of God and the future Judge of all men, even the voice of conscience was hushed to silence, and that fear of punishment gave place to joyous expectation of eternal life. But this explanation, sufficient as it is in its place, requires to be itself explained. How came it that Christ made on the mind of Paul the profound impression which we see reflected on every page of his epistles? What had the Galilean done to lead captive in willing bondage and humble reverence a man so strong in intelligence and influence as the great Apostle to the Gentiles? Certainly Christ had done something infinitely greater than Paul could do, and greater than Paul believed that any man could do. The same question must be repeated in reference to all the early followers of Christ so far as they are known to us.

The answer is not far to seek. Paul tells us plainly and again and again that his faith in Christ rested upon his belief that Christ had risen from the dead. Evidently this belief moulded his entire thought about Christ. It was the immoveable foundation of all his hopes and the ever-present inspiration of his life.

As examples I may quote Rom. i. 4, "Who was marked out as Son of God, by resurrection of the dead;" ch. iv. 24, 25, "Who believe on Him that raised Jesus our Lord from the dead, who was given up because of our trespasses and was raised because of our justification;" ch. vi. 4, "That just as Christ was raised from the dead . . . so also we may walk in newness of life;" ch. vii. 4, "That we may be given to another, even to Him that was raised from the dead;" ch. viii. 34, "Christ who died, or rather was raised;" ch. x. 9, "If thou shalt believe in thy heart that God raised Him from the dead, thou shalt be saved;" ch. xiv. 9, "To this end Christ both died and lived, that both of dead and living He may become Lord." In 1 Cor. xv., Paul reminds the Corinthian Christians that he announced to them, as one of the first principles of his gospel, that Christ had risen. He then mentions appearances of the Risen One to known persons. He goes on to say in vers. 14–19 that if Christ be not risen both his preaching and his readers' faith are vain, that he is found out to have borne false witness against God, that they are still in their sins, and that their dead companions are lost. All this proves that the resurrection of Christ was an integral part of Paul's preaching, and that his belief that He had risen was the foundation of his own and his readers' belief of the Gospel. "The life of Jesus" in 2 Cor. iv. 10, 11, is evidently explained by ver. 14: "Knowing that He who raised up the Lord Jesus will raise also us with Jesus." Notice also ch. v. 15: "May live for Him who on their behalf died and rose." To the Galatians Paul writes (ch. i. 1), as "an apostle not from men nor by man but by Jesus Christ and God the Father who raised Him from the dead."

The phrase "raised from the dead," literally "raised from among dead ones," implies clearly a bodily removal from the number of the dead. The whole argument of 1 Cor. xv. assumes that Christ rose, not merely in a spiritual sense, but in a sense incompatible with a denial of a general resurrection at the last day. And from vers. 35–49 we learn clearly that the denial referred to bodily removal from the grave: "With what body do they come? ... It is sown a natural body, it is raised a spiritual body." It is therefore quite certain that Paul shared to the full the belief embodied in the four Gospels, each of which speaks of the empty grave and of the living and risen body of Christ.

That Paul's faith was shared by others, we learn, in addition to the testimony of the four Gospels, from a letter received with confidence in the second century as written by the Apostle Peter. In 1 Pet. i. 3, we read: "Blessed be God, the Father of our Lord Jesus Christ, who ... hath begotten us again to a living hope by the resurrection of Christ from the dead." So in ver. 21: "Who through Him believe in God who raised Him from the dead, and gave Him glory, so that your faith and hope should be in God." In Acts ii. 32, Peter is recorded to have said: "This Jesus God hath raised; of which we all are witnesses." So, ch. iii. 15, almost in the same words.

Similarly, the Epistles of Paul are confirmed by His words recorded in Acts xvii. 31: "He hath set a day in which He will judge the world in righteousness by a man whom He hath ordained, having given assurance to all by raising Him from the dead. So in Acts xiii. 31: "God raised Him from the dead, who appeared for many days to those who went up with Him from Galilee to Jerusalem, who are His witnesses to the people. And again in ch. xxvi. 23: "That He first by resurrection of the dead will announce light to the people and to the nations."

These close coincidences in teaching between the Epistles of Peter and of Paul and the Book of Acts confirm strongly the tradition, accepted in the second century without a shadow of doubt, that this last was written by a friend and companion of the Apostles.

The above quotations prove that Paul and the early Christians believed that Christ rose from the dead in a way which gave absolute proof of His divine mission; and believed that God raised Him from the dead with the definite purpose that His resurrection might be the immoveable foundation of His people's faith.

The complete confidence with which Paul accepted as true, on the mere word of Christ, the stupendous promises of the Gospel, and the profound reverence with which he bowed before the supreme majesty of Christ, are now in a measure explained. Or, rather, our explanation has advanced one step. If Paul believed that Christ rose from the dead, not raised by another man but directly by the hand of God, we understand his homage to and confidence in Christ. The Conqueror of Death, of the dread potentate before whom all human distinctions fade and all human strength is vain, is indeed immeasurably greater than the greatest of men. Well might Paul believe that He occupies a relation to God shared by no other, and that He will both raise and judge the dead. And, if he believed that Christ had come back in triumph from the grave in order to proclaim eternal life to men trembling under the shadow of death, we wonder not that Paul's reverence burst forth into confidence and loyalty and love. In other words, the belief by Paul and his companions that Christ rose from the dead explains their unique reverence for Him as infinitely greater than men, and their complete confidence that the good news announced by Him is true.

Such is the result of our examination of the Christian

documents. We turned to them in order to learn something definite about the unique impulse which has left so broad and deep a mark on the past history and the present state of our race, and about the unique Person to whom that impulse was undoubtedly due. What we sought for, we have found. We have examined letters written by the most conspicuous of the immediate followers of Christ to early Christian Churches. With these we have compared very early memoirs of the life of Christ and a consecutive narrative of the planting of Christianity. The complete difference between these documents in phraseology and modes of thought assured us that they were independent witnesses. Yet their evidence about Christ was in complete harmony. And it was as confident as unanimous. This confident unanimity was to us complete proof that the distinctive elements of the teaching of the New Testament came actually from the lips of Christ. We also found proof that this teaching was accepted without doubt by the early Christians, because they looked upon Christ as immeasurably greater than man. The reverent and harmonious teaching of the different writers of the New Testament about Christ assured us that the homage paid to Him was but an acknowledgment of His own claims. Lastly, we found complete proof that the faith of the early preachers of the Gospel was based upon their firm conviction that their Master had risen from the dead.

It will be noticed that these results have been attained by methods strictly historic. We have in nowise assumed the infallibility or the divine authority of the Bible. Our conclusions have been derived, not from authoritative statements, but from the agreement of independent witnesses in circumstances which made agreement in error impossible. By similar methods we might, where sufficient evidence is accessible, determine the teaching and the claims of any other religious teacher ancient or modern. Indeed, this has already been done for all the great teachers of the world.

Comparison reveals the fact that the teaching and the personal claims of Christ are unique in the history of the world. The Koran, which we may accept as correctly reproducing the teaching of Mohammed, contains no satisfactory promise of forgiveness, or of spiritual and moral strength to break the inward bondage of sin. Nor does it claim for Mohammed superhuman dignity. On the day of his death Omar declared that he was only gone for a time and would return. But later in the day, with more wisdom, Abu Bekr, Mohammed's successor, said, "Let him that worshippeth Mohammed know that Mohammed indeed is dead: but whoso worshippeth God, let him know that the Lord liveth and doth not die." The next day Omar himself in the mosque spoke in the same strain, adding, " And truly the Inspired Word (the Koran) which directed your prophet is with us still.' [1] But neither he nor his companions claimed the living presence of their dead leader.

A closer parallel to Christ may be found in Gautama Buddha. Unfortunately, the story and the teaching of Buddha are acknowledged by his chroniclers to have been handed down as an unwritten tradition for some three hundred years. We have not, therefore, in this case the confidence derived from the contemporary Christian and

[1] See Muir's *Life of Mahomet*, new abridged ed. p. 512.

Moslem records. There is, however, reason to believe that the traditional teaching is substantially correct.

In the *Mahavagga*,[1] bk. i. 6. 8, we read: "The Blessed One addressed him in the following lines, 'I have overcome all foes, I am all-wise, I am free from stains in every way, I have left everything and have obtained emancipation by the destruction of desire. Having myself gained knowledge, whom should I call my master? I have no teacher; no one is equal to me; in the world of men and of gods no being is like me. I am the holy One in this world, I am the highest teacher, I alone am the absolute Sambuddha; I have gained coolness (by the extinction of all passion) and have obtained Nirvana. To found the Kingdom of Truth I go to the city of Benares; I will beat the drum of the immortal in the darkness of this world.'" And much else in the same strain.

In view of these claims, it is worthy of note that to Hindu thought the doctrine of Transmigration had broken down all demarcation between human and superhuman. In future lives men may become gods or animals, and gods or animals may become men. Moreover, Buddha disclaims all belief in a superhuman Ruler or Helper or Saviour. His teaching is that each one must save himself. Consequently his claim to superiority is only a denial that there exists any one greater than himself.[2]

In the Sacred Canon, *e.g. Mahavagga*, bk. i. 15–21, miraculous powers are attributed to Buddha. But his

---

[1] See Vol. xiii. of the *Sacred Books of the East*.

[2] A very interesting account of Buddhism by a modern Buddhist monk is the *Buddhistischer Katechismus*, by Subhadra Bickshu, published by Schwetschke of Brunswick.

miracles are not appealed to by himself, and apparently not by others, as proofs of his authority as a teacher.

With the story of the death and resurrection of Christ may be compared, from the Buddhist Canon, the *Book of the Great Decease*,[1] which gives a full account of the death of Buddha. No contrast could be greater. The only ray of light is that to him death is escape from the evils of existence. The only promise to his disciples is, "The truths and the rules of the order (of monks) which I have set forth and laid down for you all, let them, after I am gone, be the Teacher to you."

To the evidence found in our own inner life, in the material world, in the present relative positions and the past history of the religions of the world, must now be added the unique claims made by Christ, the unique homage paid to Him by His earliest disciples, and their confident belief that He had risen from the dead.

[1] See Vol. xi. of the same Series.

SECTION VI.

THE HISTORICAL ARGUMENT.

SUCH is our evidence. What does it prove?

The facts collected above require a restatement of the question before us. Our contemplation of the image of Christ as portrayed in the New Testament, in the presence of the Judge Supreme enthroned in our hearts, has revealed our own deep sin, and has filled us with fear of punishment. We have endeavoured to imitate this lofty ideal. But our earnest effort has only revealed our moral helplessness. For us therefore there can be no hope beyond the grave and no present peace except through forgiveness of past sins and through deliverance from a bondage which our own moral strength is powerless to break.

We have found as matter of historic fact that Jesus of Nazareth proclaimed forgiveness and moral liberation for all who believe His words. He thus claimed an authority equal to the supreme authority which condemned us. If we can find proof that His claim is just, and find reasonable grounds for assured belief that He will fulfil His promises, our deep need is supplied. But, inasmuch as no other teacher, so far as we know, has promised deliverance from the penalty and the power of sin, if such proof fail us, we have no hope.

We have also found proof that the early followers of Christ believed that His body laid dead in the grave was raised to life and that God raised Him in order thus to attest His supreme authority and the truth of the Gospel He proclaimed. If their belief was correct, Christ possessed the authority He claimed, and our hope rests on an immoveable foundation. But nothing less than manifest victory over death or some other revelation of a power greater than the ordinary forces at work around and within us can afford the proof we need. Consequently, the question with which we started is now narrowed down to one simple issue, Was the dead body of Christ raised to life? Upon this matter of historic fact depend the highest hopes of man.

It will be objected that this statement of the case brings into it a prejudice which renders impossible an impartial estimate of the evidence before us. This danger must be admitted. But it does not necessarily vitiate our judgment. Otherwise every owner of broad acres, be he ever so well versed in law, would be incapable of investigating the title-deeds of his estate. A thoughtful landowner, because of the interests at stake, scrutinises with more thoroughness the security of his tenure. So must we do. Moreover, this danger is universal. No one who has heard the Gospel is unbiassed in his judgment of it. For, if the Gospel be true, Christ claims, and claims justly, from every man unreserved devotion to Himself. They who reject this claim have a deep interest in convincing themselves either that He never made it or had no right to make it. The subtle prejudice of unbelief is the more dangerous because it is so often unsuspected. Moreover, earnest seekers for truth are often unconsciously biassed by influences arising from their history and surroundings. Our only safeguard is consciousness of our danger. In this spirit we will approach the question now before us.

It must be at once admitted that we have no proof that in modern times a dead man ever returned to life. On the other hand, around the memories of the great fables have ever been prone to gather. These facts suggest in the present case a close sifting of our evidence.

The idea of resurrection of the dead was not unknown in the days of Christ. This we learn from a suggestion of Herod Antipas and others in Matt. xiv. 2, Mark vi. 14, Luke ix. 7, that the Baptist had risen from the dead. Possibly this suggestion was prompted by the miracles recorded in 1 Kings xvii. 22, 2 Kings iv. 35. But the suggested resurrection of John differs widely from the resurrection of Christ in that the one belief vanished speedily and utterly, whereas the other gained in a few weeks thousands of adherents in the town in which Christ died, spread in a few years throughout the Roman Empire, and ultimately changed the face of the world. In each case, the rumour was tested by contact with actual facts; and with very different results.

The alternative before us, viz. that Christ did or did not rise, we shall best investigate by assuming in turn that each hypothesis is true, tracing our assumption to its logical results, and comparing these with the facts already gathered. Certain other facts and combinations of facts apparently inconsistent with the hypothesis that Christ actually rose, we will postpone to the next section.

If in very truth Christ rose from the dead, all the facts

before us are explained. For, in that case we may believe that, as narrated in Acts i. 3, He showed Himself to His disciples "in many proofs," and thus evoked in them complete confidence that their Master had trampled death under His feet. If so, we can understand the courage which set at defiance the threats and the power of the most powerful in Jerusalem. Men who on Friday saw Christ hanging on a cross or knew that He was dead, and who on Sunday saw Him living and strong, might well be fearless. For their Master was now manifestly Lord of Life and Death; and He had promised ever to be with them. Their fearless assertion that Christ had risen, in the face of men who had every motive for silencing them and apparently many means of doing so, would naturally convince many. And, that many were convinced, the survival and spread of early Christianity proves. If Christ rose, we can understand how Paul's contact with Christians while dragging them before courts of law would help his conversion. For, we can easily conceive that, as he listened to their straightforward statements of fact, and possibly to their account of the teaching of Christ, he would find it more and more difficult to resist the accumulating evidence that the Crucified One was indeed the hoped-for Deliverer. This slowly dawning and growing conviction would prepare the way for the crisis which raised it at once to complete certainty. Thus the actual resurrection of Christ would abundantly account for the early spread of Christianity.

It would also account for the effect of the Gospel upon the world. For, if Christ rose from the dead, He was what He claimed to be. And we have seen that He claimed to be in a unique sense the Son of God, the

Saviour of the world, and the future Judge of all men. If He was such, His birth was immeasurably the most stupendous event in the history of the world. And the Gospel preached by His disciples was the chosen instrument used by the infinite power of God in order to accomplish the purposes for which His Son became Man. We wonder not that they who bore this instrument of omnipotence were themselves regardless of the power of men. Nor do we wonder that their brave words wrought conviction in thousands, that the Gospel survived all efforts to silence it and the Church all efforts to destroy it, and that ultimately Christianity took among the religions of the world the place of pre-eminence it holds to-day.

On the other hand, if Christ did not rise, the belief of His early followers, and the effect of the Gospel upon the world, are incapable of explanation. They are, as we shall see, effects for which no adequate causes can be adduced; they are phenomena contradicting all the observed sequences of human life.

Indisputably, a man who was crucified at Jerusalem as a malefactor was shortly afterwards, in the city in which He died, accepted by thousands of Jews as the long and eagerly expected deliverer of their nation, because they believed that He had risen from the dead. If their belief was correct, they who crucified Him had slain the Hope of Israel. They were guilty of the blood not so much of a man as of a nation. If this were once believed, the lives of the murderers of Christ were not worth a day's purchase. How real was their danger we learn from Acts v. 26, where we read that the servants of the High-priestly party "feared the people, lest they should be stoned."

Evidently then the enemies of Christ had the strongest possible motive for proving that He had not risen from the dead.

Abundant means of proving it were probably within their reach. For, if He had not risen, His body would be somewhere in Jerusalem. And the burial-place of so famous a man, adored by some, hated by others, would almost certainly be known. By opening the grave, the powerful party who had slain Him would be able at once and for ever to put an end to the delusion which was spreading among the people. This easy way of escape from a great and increasing danger, we cannot conceive them neglecting. Even if the corpse were in the possession of His friends, this fact could hardly be kept from the knowledge of His enemies. Certainly, it could not without deliberate and careful concealment. But such concealment is inconceivable. A belief which the most powerful party in Jerusalem had the strongest motive and abundant means to dispel, and which nevertheless survived and spread, was not born of fraud. Nor can we conceive a few Christians knowing the facts and concealing them from the rest. If the body of Christ remained dead in Jerusalem, the Apostles must have known it. If they had known it, they could not have spread through the Roman Empire the belief that He had risen.

In any case, even if the corpse of Jesus had utterly vanished from the view of friends and foes, a most unlikely supposition, the enemies of Christ had abundant means of silencing all public announcement that He had risen. That they were unable to silence, even by the threat or infliction of death, a definite rumour touching plain matter of fact which exposed them to deadly peril, is strong presumption that the rumour was true. In other words, the survival and spread of Christianity cannot with any likelihood be explained except on the supposition that Christ rose from the dead.

Nor can the conversion of Paul. For his intelligence, sharpened by hostility, would detect the baselessness of a belief resting only on the imagination and credulity of unlettered men and women. That he did not detect its baselessness, but on the contrary accepted the belief of the Galileans as his own deep conviction, proves that he had what seemed to him complete evidence that He whose followers he had so bitterly persecuted had indeed risen from the dead and was the hoped-for deliverer of Israel. Evidence sufficient to convince so determined an enemy bears on its front the mark of truth.

Our strongest historical argument remains. If Christ did not rise, a delusion has saved the world.

In the days of Christ, the apparently hopeless world was sinking helplessly into social chaos. Gradually, out of the chaos we have seen new life rising, until at last it has nearly overspread the earth. The nations which have received it stand to-day in the front rank. And to these the most hopeful of other nations are looking for help. Even in the social life of our own country we see the moral influence of Christianity. If these influences were removed, there would be in modern life a void which nothing could fill.

All these results have flowed from the preaching of men who, but for the courage inspired by a belief that their Master had risen from the dead, would never have dared to preach, or certainly would not have devoted their lives to the unwearied proclamation of the Gospel. Especially are these results due to the preaching of one who gave proof of the strength and sincerity of his belief by forsaking in the noonday of his life the murderers of Christ and joining the company of His persecuted followers.

Now if Christ did not actually rise, this belief was a delusion. And it is the most astounding delusion that ever darkened the erring mind of man. For not only did it enable its early votaries to set at nought hardship and peril and death but in all succeeding ages it has held captive many of the most intelligent and cultured of men, and now for many centuries nearly all the best of men. Unquestionably it occupies a position without parallel among the delusions of mankind.

That delusion has saved the world. For, as we have seen, had not the early preachers of the Gospel been deluded about the historic fact of the resurrection of Christ, they would never have preached, there would have been no Christian Churches and no Christianity, the one influence which has saved the world from ruin would not have existed, and the world would have perished.

If this be so, we owe to delusion and to error a debt greater than we can conceive.

Fortunate it was for the world that the early Christians were so easily deceived by the creations of their own imagination. Had Peter and John been men of cooler and keener intelligence, instead of preaching that Christ had risen, they would have sought out His grave and found that His body was still there, or they would have found that it had never been given to His friends (as is stated expressly in each of the four Gospels) but had become indistinguishable in some trench in which the other criminals were buried. Then would the triumph of Annas and Caiaphas have been complete. The Galileans would have crept back to their fishing, and Jesus would have been remembered only as the last and the greatest of the murdered prophets.

Fortunate it was for the world that the scholar of Gamaliel was so easily led astray by the fishermen of Gennesaret. If the author of the Epistle to the Romans had been armed with the keen weapons of modern historical criticism, he would not only have escaped, but have done much to dispel, the delusion to which he fell a victim. For he would have persecuted the Christians to the end; or, if he had come to a better mind, would have explained to Peter and John that the real grandeur of Christ lay not in His supposed resurrection from the dead and superhuman dignity but in the purity of His life and the loftiness of His moral teaching. Or, more likely, he would have pointed them to the closed grave in which their Lord lay dead. The result, we can conjecture. In that grave, amid the ridicule of the enemies of Christ, would have been buried the hope of the world.

A plain alternative is now before us. If Christ did not rise, in a manner revealing the presence of a power greater than the known forces of the material world and thus proving the justness of His stupendous claims, a delusion has turned back the entire current of human history and saved the world. If so, in the greatest crisis of the world's history, delusion has been better than knowledge and error better than truth.

If we accept this supposition, we may well be pardoned if we prefer delusion to knowledge, error to truth.

Note now the logical consequence of the only alternative open to those who deny or doubt that Christ rose from the dead. In all ages men have sought knowledge, and some have made it, under many difficulties, the chief aim of life, in a belief that TO KNOW THE TRUTH is for man's highest interest, and that the Truth is able to repay any price at which it may be purchased. The Majesty of Truth is now dethroned. For we have seen that it may be either a gain or possibly an infinite injury. This uncertainty makes knowledge unworthy of serious effort, especially of prolonged and difficult and costly effort. Thus in the closed grave of Christ is buried, not only the world's hope, but the chief stimulus for intelligent research.

It is quite true that occasionally and on a small scale partial knowledge has been injurious and error beneficial. We keep back from a sick man bad news, fearing th t it may do him harm. But we do this only because his condition is abnormal, well knowing that if he recover he will learn all. On the stage of history the case of Joan of Arc may be quoted as one in which religious delusion wrought national deliverance. But here the chief delusion was in the French nation which had fallen a victim to the strange error of supposing itself unable to expel from its soil a handful of invaders. Joan grasped, with true prophetic insight, the great truth that the God of nations was on the side of France, and that He designed her nation to be free. This faith, her disposition and training robed in the form of visions. But she made no assertions which could be demonstrated to be historically false. Her own firm faith, even associated with a measure of delusion, was strong enough to dispel a more serious delusion, and thus to save France. But, if Joan had never lived, we cannot doubt that in some way the nation would have woke up to a consciousness of its strength, and have shaken off the yoke of bondage.

The success of Buddha, and that of Mohammed, may be quoted. But neither of these men based his claim on erroneous statements of fact, or at least not on statements capable of disproof. Mohammed definitely disowned miracles as proofs of his divine mission. In the Sacred Canon of the Buddhists we read of many miracles wrought by Buddha. See above, p. 117. And he claims absolute authority as a moral teacher. But he does not appeal to his miracles in proof of his authority: nor are we told that his disciples accepted his authority because of his miracles. We have in the Buddhist records nothing parallel to Mark ii. 10, 11; John ii. 11, iii. 2, iv. 53, ix. 30–33, xi. 48, xx. 28, 29; Acts ii. 22, 32, iii. 15, iv. 10, x. 38, 39. Indeed, the teaching of Mohammed and Buddha needed no miraculous credentials. For, so far as in each case it was true, it appealed at once to their hearers' moral judgment. And this was its power. But these teachers did not attempt to show a way of forgiveness for past sins, nor did they promise power over sin. The faith of their followers thus differs altogether from the belief of the early Christians that their Master had risen from the grave and had therefore authority on earth to forgive sins.

We have now seen that to deny or doubt the resurrection of Christ is to believe, or to believe possible, that

Christianity is a fortunate accident; and that a delusion born of religious excitement has done more for our race than all the intelligent effort of man. And we have seen that this suggestion if accepted would overturn a deep-seated and very beneficial belief underlying all human thought and life, namely that Knowledge and Truth are better than ignorance and error. Certainly they who deny or doubt the actual and bodily resurrection of Christ[1] are bound to show that it lies open to objections more serious than those which lie against the logical consequences of their own denial or doubt,—that it violates some law greater than that which their own denial overturns.

These objections we will now consider.

[1] See Note v., on *Biblical Rationalism*.

SECTION VII.

OBJECTIONS.

To the foregoing argument, it cannot be objected that the Bible contains statements highly incredible or indisputably untrue. For I have neither assumed, nor endeavoured to prove, the general truthfulness of the Bible. But we have found abundant and indisputable proof that certain parts of it were written, in a form practically the same as that which we now possess, by the Apostle Paul. Therefore, apart from the correctness or error of the rest of the Bible, we are sure that they reflect correctly his mind and thought. And, as we have seen, they prove beyond possibility of doubt that he believed Christ to be the Eternal Son of God, and believed that the body of Christ laid dead in the grave returned to life. Moreover, whatever be the date or authority of the other documents of the New Testament, their unanimous agreement affords complete proof that Paul's belief was shared by the early followers of Christ. Indeed, only thus can we account for the belief of Paul. In other words, the literary facts of the New Testament can be accounted for only by supposing that all the early followers of Christ believed without a shadow of doubt that their Master had risen from the dead. This argument is not touched by the unlikeliness of any other statements contained in the Bible. Each of these must be discussed on its own merits.

Nor is our argument invalidated by any apparent or real discrepancies between the accounts of the resurrection given in the Four Gospels. For it rests, not upon the Gospels, but primarily upon Paul's manifest belief that Christ rose from the dead. These discrepancies do nothing to account for the Apostles' belief, for its effect upon themselves, and through them upon the world. On the other hand, the discrepancies are easily accounted for by the frequent incorrectness of human observation, recollection, or testimony. This explanation is the more easy because of the excitement of the moment and the hurrying to and fro of those who had seen the empty grave and thought they had seen a vision of angels. And they bear witness to the independence of the four narratives.

It is worthy of note that amid many differences there are important points in which our four narratives of the resurrection agree. They all say that on the morning but one after the death of Christ, which was the day after the Jewish Sabbath, Mary of Magdala, alone or accompanied by other women, came to the grave and found it empty. The Third and Fourth Gospels say that on the evening of the same day Jesus appeared to His assembled disciples, in a way which assured them that He had risen from the grave. The First Gospel and what seems to be a fragment appended to the Second say that on the morning of the same day He appeared to one or more women. This agreement proves that the belief of the resurrection had its birth, not in Galilee, but at Jerusalem, and within three days of His death.

If the foregoing historical argument is not overturned by historical inaccuracies in small details of the Christian documents, still less is it weakened by statements in the Bible apparently inconsistent with modern science. Indeed, such statements do not affect the historic truth even of the documents in which they are found. For a man who accepts current mistakes about the phenomena of nature may yet be a reliable witness touching matters of fact. The books of Holy Scripture were not written to teach natural science. We have therefore no right to expect in them scientific accuracy above that of the age in which they were composed.[1]

Nor is ground of objection found in the defective moral tone of a few passages in the Bible. The lofty morality of the entire New Testament, and the vast moral and spiritual superiority of the Old Testament to the ages in which it was written, go far to confirm the truthfulness of its historical statements. For men who could write thus would not willingly deceive. Certainly the few passages of the Old Testament which breathe a spirit we should not now approve can do nothing to weaken an argument based upon the belief of the Apostles, men whose character evokes our highest admiration.

The historic truthfulness and the moral authority of Holy Scripture lie outside the scope of the present lecture. I have not appealed, nor can I fairly appeal, to the authority of the Bible in proof that Christ claimed unique dignity, or in proof that He rose from the dead. For no one will accept the authority of the Bible as decisive who does not first admit this claim and believe this historic

---

[1] See Note iv., on *The Bible and Science.*

fact. Moreover, the appeal is needless. For, without attributing to Holy Scripture any special authority, and sifting the evidence it affords as we should that of any other ancient document, we have already found proof that Christ claimed to be the Eternal Son of God, and in proof of His claim came forth living from the grave.

No subject in our day within the range of theology is in greater need of elucidation than that of the origin and authority of Holy Scripture. Earlier treatises have been in some measure superseded by literary facts recently brought to light. The bearing of these facts upon the authority of the Bible calls loudly for investigation. But all such investigation must rest, for the reason just given, upon prior proof of the great historical facts of Christianity. It can be successfully accomplished only by a competent scholar acquainted with, and able to appreciate, the results of modern Biblical research, and in full sympathy with the spiritual aim of the Gospel of Christ.

A more serious objection, not to the foregoing historical proof but to that which it is designed to prove, now demands attention. Not a few modern scholars, some of them very able and widely familiar with the Christian documents, refuse to discuss any historical proof that Christ rose from the dead, assuming with complete confidence as self-evident that resurrection of a dead man is absolutely impossible. This assumption implies that to the actual resurrection of Christ there are objections outweighing far the strong historical proof just adduced. The scholars to whom I refer quote the discrepancies, apparent or real, of the narratives of the resurrection as discrediting their testimony: and some of them point to the extreme unlikeliness of some other statements in the Bible.[1] But these are not the real reasons of their confident rejection of all evidence that Christ came forth living from the grave. It rests upon other grounds: and these demand now our most serious attention.

To those who endeavour to prove that Christ rose from the dead, it is replied, as a triumphant disproof, that "miracles do not happen." It is boldly asserted that the return to life of a dead man would be a breach in the uniform operation of the laws of nature, that upon this recognised uniformity rest all human science and philosophy and all material progress, and that to admit the possibility of its interruption would be to surrender the foundation of modern civilisation.

This objection rests entirely upon the assumption that that which does not happen before the eyes of men to-day never happened since the world began to be, that the already observed sequences are the only existing sequences, and that the only forces influencing our universe are those revealing themselves day by day in the phenomena around us.

This assumption is not only without proof but is utterly disproved by the material history of our planet as written in plain characters before our eyes. For, as we have already seen, all students of natural science admit that at some time in the past, suddenly or gradually, where before all was lifeless life began to be. Such transition now from lifelessness to life, the utmost scientific scrutiny has failed to detect. Nor do the uniform sequences already observed present any parallel to it. The first

---

[1] See Note v., on *Biblical Rationalism*.

origin of the carbon compounds cannot be explained by the laws of chemical affinity. And between these compounds as chemical combinations and organized living matter capable of assimilating to itself and within itself other matter and thus growing and propagating its kind there are chasms which even imagination utterly fails to span. Yet indisputably, as matter of fact, these chasms have actually been spanned. Reality has overleaped a gulf which imagination dares not attempt. In other words, something which never happens now happened in an age gone by. This reveals the operation then of a force never, so far as we know, operating within the memory of man.

This force and the mode of its operation are inconceivable; *i.e.* they cannot be grasped by the human mind. From this we learn that the inconceivable may yet be actual, and be known. We know, *i.e.* we have intelligible and sufficient reasons for certainty, that this force operated in the past; and we know something about it, namely that it was a force capable of producing life out of the lifeless. Thus a matter which in its mode of existence and of operation is inconceivable may yet be in some respects an object of knowledge.

The origin of life is as much and as little inconsistent with the uniform operation of natural law as is the resurrection of Christ. Neither event implies a moment's suspension of the forces previously at work in the material world. But each reveals the presence of a power higher than those previously observed or observable and producing phenomena altogether different from all earlier phenomena. We can well conceive, before life began, the forces of gravitation, light, heat, electricity, and chemical affinity operating according to the laws since observed by men. We are compelled to believe that in the midst of these already operating forces a new force began to operate, neutralising apparently, and certainly modifying the operation of, the forces already at work. But the earlier forces continued to operate, and modified the action of the new forces. Living bodies are influenced, and to a large extent controlled, by gravitation. Yet whenever we lift a weight we produce a locomotion which is a resistance of gravitation. But that even while we do so the force of gravitation is by no means suspended, the weariness of our arm testifies. Similarly, our bodies are subject to, and indeed are kept alive by, the operation of chemical affinities. Yet the vital force within us neutralises chemical forces which, left to themselves by the absence of life, would dissolve our bodies. The origin of life affords no evidence of any break whatever in the unform operation of the laws of nature: but it affords complete proof of the operation formerly of a force never seen in operation now and producing results altogether unlike the phenomena now observed, viz. the force which, apart from pre-existent life, drew together the lifeless chemical atoms of the inorganic world, formed them into new combinations, and breathed into them life. The advent of this new force created a new era in the history of our planet, an era not only surpassing infinitely all previous eras, but giving to them as preparatory to this new development a significance without which they would have been meaningless and worthless.

Similarly, the history of our race bears witness that in Jesus of Nazareth there was at work a moral force altogether unlike the moral forces observed in other men. In His day society was rapidly gravitating to ruin. Within the Roman Empire corruption ran riot without a parallel in the worst subsequent ages. In the east were ancient and powerless civilisations already worn out; in the north, the chaos of barbarism. To the most thoughtful men scarcely a ray of hope appeared. Unexpectedly, and imperceptibly, an unseen hand arrested the apparently inevitable ruin. Amid the corruption of the decaying and falling empire, germs of new life appeared and began to grow. These found congenial soil among the rough but manly races of the north. And now, for more than a thousand years, from these germs has been growing the noble tree of modern European life, under whose spreading branches morality and culture and prosperity have found shelter. This new moral impulse, producing results so great, was a phenomenon utterly unlike everything else in the world's history. Indisputably it had its root in Jesus of Nazareth. And it reveals a moral force operating in and through Him which cannot be classed among other moral forces observed at work during the history of our race.

We are not surprised to find this new moral force affecting directly the operation of the forces of the material world. For the moral and material are so closely related that what affects one affects also the other. We therefore need not wonder that, in the human body of Him whose influence arrested the rapidly advancing moral corruption of our race, was arrested also the material corruption which in all others follows death, that even the hand of death was compelled to release its prey and that the Dead One came forth living from the grave. This by no means implies a suspension of the operation of those chemical forces which reduce, in all dead men, into simpler compounds the very complex compounds which compose organic bodies. It implies only that in the sacred body of Jesus was present a life higher than the life which lives in us, that this higher life was stronger than death, and that it held back, or rolled back, the forces of decay operating now in all the dead, and made what in others would have been a final separation of body and spirit to be but a transient sleep. Admit once that there are in the world forces other and higher than those revealed in the observed sequences of the material world, and we need not wonder if we find here and there phenomena which cannot be classed among these ordinary sequences. Such phenomena we have in the origin of life and in the origin of Christianity. In each case, the new phenomenon opened a new era in the world's history.

Another such era, apparently, was the origin of motion. For the world is full of movements which cannot be accounted for by gravitation or chemical affinity or any of the forces inherent in matter. They therefore imply an original impulse or impulses in a direction other than that of the inherent forces. Moreover, these forces do not account for the heterogeneity of the universe. Had matter been originally homogeneous, and had there been no impulse from without, it would have remained homogeneous. Now it is difficult to conceive matter originally heteregeneous. For heterogeneity must have a definite form. And this we can hardly conceive without pre-existent conditions; which an original form cannot have.

That impulse, which must have taken place, whether or not matter had a still earlier existence, we may perhaps look upon as the first moment of time. For from that moment began the sequence of earlier and later.

It is not difficult to trace in the history of our planet the advent of another new force creating another new era. No influences known to be at work in the animal world bridge over, or even tend to bridge, the infinite distance between the mechanical instincts of the highest brutes and the moral sense and capacity for improvement of even the lowest men.[1] Moreover, the course of human history does not favour the supposition that the earliest races of men were the lowest. We have no record of a savage race rising into culture apart from the influence of existing cultured races. The self-development of barbarism into culture is one of the events which "do not happen." Unless the earlier history of our race differs immensely from all later history, the beginning of human life spanned a chasm far wider than that which separates the highest from the lowest animals. In a world peopled only by brutes, reasoning man began to be. The birth of reason reveals the operation of a force altogether new on earth, a force which created a new era and gave to life an importance unknown before. Yet, as in the former cases, this new impulse did not in any way suspend the operation of the earlier forces. Intelligent human life is subject to gravitation, chemical affinity, and the mysterious laws of animal life; while yet frequently diverting their operation into new channels.

The rarity of the new impulses noted above warns us

[1] See p. 52.

not to accept without most careful scrutiny phenomena apparently new as evidence of the operation of a force hitherto unknown. This inference is allowable only where we have abundant and various facts widely and thoroughly known, and where the observed phenomena differ in kind from all the observed results of known forces. Such abundant facts, as already seen, we have in the origin of life and in the origin of Christianity. Around each of these events we find phenomena utterly inexplicable by the forces at work in the pre-existent inorganic world and in social life before Christ. Similar proof we find in the origin of motion, and of reason.

This argument by no means implies that we are able to measure the possibilities of the forces at work in inorganic matter and in the ages preceding the birth of Christ. In an old story, a shipwrecked mariner took heart because he saw on the shore geometrical figures which revealed to him the presence of intelligent men. Not that he could determine exactly what lines the wind and the waves, or wild animals, could trace on the sand. He knew at once and knew well that the lines he saw were utterly beyond the power of such agencies. Similarly in the history of our planet written on the page of nature, and in the history of our race, we see effects which all the known natural and social forces are unable to produce.

Successive epochs in the history of the world need create no surprise. In the microcosm of each individual life we have marked stages of development. And such we have found in the macrocosm of the great universe. The Christian looks for a still more glorious epoch in the future, when the material universe itself, which bears already marks of decay, shall give place to the eternal home of the children of God.

Scarcely worthy of mention is the objection that many supposed miracles have long ago been found to be mere human fancies or unusual effects of ordinary causes. That many rumours are untrue, is no reason for neglecting all rumour as worthless; but warns us not to accept rumours without due investigation. Scrutiny separates the true from the false.

In view of all this, we may fairly claim full proof before accepting as true the miraculous stories of the New Testament. But we have no right, prior to investigation, to reject them as false. Such proof, for the resurrection of Christ, I have endeavoured to bring. The sufficiency of it, each reader must judge for himself.

One more objection deserves notice. It is said that the slow progress of Christianity and the many defects of Christian nations and Christian Churches disprove the divine origin of the Gospel and the divinity of Christ; that if God had designed men to be Christians He would have given proof banishing all doubt from all minds, and have brought to bear on all men influences which would have led them to bow to Christ. It must be admitted that in spite of the Gospel a great part of the human race is still non-Christian, and that even among Christians very much exists utterly alien from the spirit of Christ. To some men this seems to be conclusive proof that the Gospel does not come from an Almighty Being.

Possibly, if we had God's power, along with our own ignorance, we should be unable to refrain from forcing our will upon all our creatures. But it is by no means certain that this would be for their good. Irresistible intellectual proof and irresistible moral influences would destroy human freedom and reduce men to mere machines. Thus would mankind be deprived of its noblest prerogative, and human life of its distinctive worth. Better to have a race of freemen of whom, as is now the case, an increasing number deliberately and resolutely choose the right, rather than a race incapable of choice and therefore of good or evil. To assume that God must needs, at this cost, force His will upon men, is absurd. And if so, the slow and partial effect of the Gospel does not afford even the slightest presumption that it is not divine.

That man is actually free and that his destiny is in his own hands, we have already inferred from his sense of freedom, which is too strong and widespread to be a delusion, and from the moral injury resulting inevitably from denial of his freedom. And if God thought fit to make man free, we wonder not that even in His purpose of mercy He respects the freedom thus given, and permits man to refuse the offered mercy. Admit this, and all is explained. Because man is free, the progress of Christianity has been hindered by all the influences which darken the mind and warp the right action of man. Because the Gospel is divine, it has surmounted all obstacles which bad men have thrown across its path, has cast aside many corruptions derived from the human imperfections of its advocates and adherents, and is purer and stronger to-day than ever before. In other words, the new life in Christ is moulded in its development by the various forces already operating in man's moral and social life. Hence its slow progress and partial reception.

This slow and somewhat fitful development, hindered by pre-existent influences, is not peculiar to Christianity. Slow and chequered was the development of spiritual life under the Old Covenant. But it attained its goal as a needful and effective preparation for the Gospel of Christ. Still slower was the early development of vegetable and animal life, moulded and in some measure controlled by pre-existent inorganic forces. At its first dawn and for long ages life gave no promise of what it was afterwards to become. And the rude forces of lifeless matter threatened to destroy it. But life survived and grew and developed in marvellous variety, and clothed the world with myriad forms of beauty.

Thus in each of its great formative epochs the story of our planet and of the known universe presents the same features. Amid pre-existent forces, once and again new life appears with new laws of its own. Along these new lines, yet modified by existing forces, the new life has developed until at length it has transformed and ennobled everything around.

We have in this section admitted that a conspicuous and important and pervasive element in the Christian documents, viz. the many assertions that Christ rose from the dead, contradicts at first sight the teaching of the Book of Nature. So serious has this contradiction seemed to not a few careful students both of the Christian documents and of the material world that they have brought themselves to believe, in deference to their reading of Natural Science, that all the early followers of Christ have in several important points been in error, and have seriously misrepresented their Master's teaching about Himself and about the way of salvation. But we have now seen that this suggestion of despair is needless. Between the voice of nature even as expounded by many who reject the recorded teaching of Christ, and the Christian documents, there is perfect harmony. For Nature bears on her breast the record of one or more events as unlike her ordinary course as is the resurrection of Christ. They who read that record find in it nothing which need compel them to accept the only possible alternative, viz. that a delusion has saved the world; and to reject the abundant evidence on which rests the Christian hope.

SECTION VIII.

THE RESULT.

From various sources we have gathered facts bearing upon the truth of the Gospel of Christ. The combined weight of this manifold evidence, we must now endeavour to estimate.

It has often been said that most Christians accept the Gospel merely because they have been taught it from childhood by teachers whom they have been trained to respect. And the fact that many of them have not personally examined the historic evidence for Christianity has seemed to give colour to this statement. It is as much and as little true as would be the assertion that we accept the theory of gravitation because it was taught by Newton. If neither he nor any one else had discovered the law of gravitation, and had it not been taught us, we should not now believe it. But this is by no means the reason of our belief. Unable as we are to discover by our own researches Newton's great generalisation, we are able to understand the proofs on which it rests. And these proofs would remain in full force, and our belief in gravitation would be unchanged, even if historical criticism overturned every supposed fact of Newton's life. We accept the theory of gravitation because it explains a multitude of facts otherwise inexplicable.

For similar reasons the followers of Christ believe the Gospel and the statements of fact on which it rests. These facts and this Gospel they heard in childhood from lips to which they were accustomed to listen with reverence. What they heard then with childlike confidence they believe now in the mature thought of manhood, because it explains, and is to them the only conceivable explanation of, a multitude of facts brought under their observation by the manifold experiences of life. These facts they find in the secret thought of their own hearts, in the social life of their fellowmen, and even in the material world. This evidence accumulates day by day. And each fresh experience is additional verification of the one theory which gives to the phenomena of life unity and intelligibility.

The Christian faith may be thus stated. We believe that the visible universe and ourselves were made and are now controlled by an intelligent and loving Creator, Himself without beginning; that with Him from eternity is One personally distinct from Him yet sharing to the full His infinite knowledge and power and love, the Eternal Son of God; that in order to save and bless the whole race God joined to Himself in unique alliance, and enriched with special knowledge of Himself, one ancient nation; that for the same end and in this sacred nation the Eternal Son assumed human form and lived a man among men; that He announced eternal life for all who should believe and obey Him; that, in order to harmonise the pardon of sinners with the justice of God, He submitted to die; that He rose from the dead and ascended to heaven; that from His throne the Risen Lord anointed His followers with His own power and with the Spirit of God that they might carry to the ends of the earth the good news of salvation and eternal life; and that He will return to raise the dead and to judge all men.

This we may call the Christian Theory. We accept it because it explains the most important phenomena known to us, because it does not seriously conflict with known phenomena, and because it is to us the only conceivable explanation of all the facts of the case. It explains the majesty of the Moral Law, by tracing it to Him who made man in order that man might intelligently serve God and thus attain his highest welfare. It explains the moral inequalities of the present life, by announcing complete retribution beyond the grave. It explains the recognition by our moral sense of the supreme authority of the teaching and example of Christ as recorded in the New Testament. For it tells us that that record is true, and that in recognising the moral grandeur of Christ our moral sense does but bow to its Author and Lord. It explains the fitness of the Gospel to supply man's deep spiritual need. It explains the firm belief of the early followers of Christ that their Master had risen from the dead, the conversion of Paul, the transforming effect of the Gospel upon the world, and the pre-eminence of Christianity to-day among the religions of the world. It explains the singular story of Israel in its relation both to the heathen and to Christianity. It explains, in no small degree, the material universe and the mysterious origin of life, by tracing both to an unseen and competent and intelligent First Cause.

In other words, the hypothesis that Christ came forth living from the grave in which He lay dead, and that therefore He is what He claimed to be and the Gospel He announced is true, carried to its logical consequences, explains fairly and fully the facts of human life. It explains a great multitude of facts within us and around us and on the page of human history. To many Christians, increasing acquaintance with these facts has revealed with increasing clearness the completeness of the explanation offered by the Gospel.

The foregoing evidence becomes the more conclusive when we consider the only possible alternative to the Christian Theory. If Christ did not rise from the dead, we are compelled to believe that all His early followers, including the intelligent Apostle of the Gentiles, were in serious error touching the essential dignity and the supposed resurrection of their Master; that they made everywhere about Him assertions which He would Himself have rejected as blasphemy; and, strangest of all, that the delusion embodied in these assertions was the mainspring of a moral and religious impulse which saved the world from ruin and led it into a path of sustained progress. An alternative involving consequences so utterly contrary to all experience cannot be entertained for a moment unless denial of it involves consequences still more unlikely. But we have seen that the only serious objection to the theory here advocated rests upon the assumption that what does not happen now never happened since time began. And this assumption has been already disproved by the admitted facts of the material world. We therefore need not hesitate to accept with complete confidence the one theory which explains to us the manifold experiences of life.

Complete as is this proof, it is by no means the whole.

Nor is it the most conclusive. There are other facts not yet mentioned and still more decisive. Thousands of men and women have dared to believe the Gospel. They have dared to accept Christ's promise of eternal life. And in proportion to their faith they have obtained power to trample under foot sins which once held them in degrading bondage, and to live a life inward and outward which claims their own self-respect. All this is matter of direct introspection combined with memory of the past. They are immediately conscious of a hand reached out to them from above and daily raising them. We have here another moral sequence, viz. faith in Christ and victory over sin. The supreme judge within, from whose condemnation once they found no escape, now testifies, amid many remaining defects, to their upward progress. That judgment, when it condemned them, they dared not contradict. They dare not contradict it now. It is to them an absolute verification of the truth of the Gospel they have believed. That which day by day raises them, and without which they ever sink, cannot be a delusion. Else delusion would be to them, by the infallible verdict of the judge within, immensely better than truth. And if truth is opposed to morality, it has lost for ever its claim to our homage. This claim, the truth can never lose. And, therefore, that which is morally hurtful cannot be intellectually true.

This last evidence disproves the frequent assertion that the teachings of theology are incapable of verification. Theology is but an orderly and reasoned statement of whatever we know about the unseen world and man's relation to it. And, as I have endeavoured to show, some of the findings of theology are daily verified in the hearts and lives of all servants of Christ. The correct statement would be that the objectors have not themselves verified the teaching of theology. To say that they cannot be verified, is an unproved dogmatic assertion.

The error underlying this assertion is very widespread. It is a practical, though sometimes unconscious, contempt for that which has not come under our own immediate observation. Similar assertions might be made about the generalisations of natural science. To those not familiar with the facts on which they rest, some of these seem to be mere vagaries of an unbridled imagination. The atomic theory and especially attempts to calculate the weight of molecules or atoms might in this way be held up to ridicule. Such ridicule, every student of natural science rightly rejects with contempt. Unfortunately, some of them, forgetting that there are sciences other than, and very different from, their own, and facts which lie outside their own department of science, are themselves guilty of similar folly.

It is worthy of note that different men find, each in his own peculiar surroundings, peculiar yet complete evidence that the Gospel is true. To the Christian philosopher it offers an explanation of the phenomena of life which satisfies his intelligence and gives unity to his conception of the universe. To the student of history it affords a key to the strange story of the nations. To the man of business it reveals a path safe and honourable amid the dangerous whirl of commerce and leading to something better than material wealth. And to thousands in every age and rank the Gospel commends itself as true by giving them a theory of life which satisfies their intelligence, an aim in life the noblest they can conceive, and a moral strength which they know to be not human but divine. This universal applicability is the supreme test of truth.

Such are some of the reasons of the Christian hope. Let us now trace in scanty outline its practical results.

We found ourselves condemned because of our past sins by an authority from which there was no appeal: and we found ourselves held fast and held down by fetters we could not break. A voice has come to us announcing pardon. This voice we have proved to be that of the Author of our being and the Arbiter of our destiny. Before His supreme authority, the condemnation within sinks into silence, and condemnation gives place to hope. The voice of mercy promises to break our fetters: and we know that it comes from One who is able to do so. In His presence we dare not doubt. And thousands of men and women of every condition in life testify that they day by day experience the promised deliverance. To all of us life on earth is bounded by the sleep of death. But a voice from beyond the grave promises, to all who believe it, immortal life. Standing by the empty grave of Christ and beneath the shadow of the cross on which He died for our sins, we cannot doubt these glad tidings of great joy. Therefore whatever the Gospel proclaims about believers it proclaims about us. Its promises thus assure us that in that endless blessedness we have a part.

It is now evident that the Gospel gives, to those who believe it, an assured knowledge of personal salvation and a well-grounded hope of life beyond the grave. This assurance rests primarily, neither upon inward experience nor upon a consciousness of having done right, but upon doctrines and promises which we have traced by strictly historical methods to the lips of Christ, of whom we have found conclusive proof that He rose from the dead and is therefore worthy of our highest confidence. And it is verified by an inward experience which admits of no doubt, viz. by the liberation and growth of that in us which we know to be noblest and best. Thus upon the same immoveable foundation rest both our belief that the Gospel is true, our trust in Christ, and our assurance of personal salvation.

It is also evident that in the Gospel is revealed the secret of moral victory and of moral growth.

And now all is changed, and all is well. Life on earth is no longer a little hut in a wilderness surrounded at a short distance by impenetrable darkness. It is a lighted porch leading to our Father's house in heaven. The material world is a mirror in which we see reflected His face. And its fading beauty is a faint outshining of the eternal glory awaiting His children. Life on earth assumes now a new dignity. For actions wrought in bodies soon to crumble into dust will produce results abiding for ever. The only things transient and insignificant are weariness and hardship and pain and sorrow and tears. All that is good is eternal. Thus the Christian hope ennobles the humblest human life, and sheds lustre even on the material world around us.

Just as our planet lies in the bosom of the universe of stars, completely separated from them yet united to them by unseen and mysterious bonds, so human life on earth lies in the bosom of eternity, encompassed on all sides by the unseen world, completely separated from it yet linked to it in closest relationship. Some men see not or heed not the lights overhead. To them nothing is visible except the earth on which they tread or the dark and stormy waters on which their barque is tossed. These seem to them to be the only world with which they have to do. And they know not whither through the darkness they are sailing. For to them the sky is overcast. But to those who look away from earth with patient gaze, the clouds disperse. Other and greater and brighter worlds appear; and our earth is seen to be but a small part of one vast universe, and life on earth to be but the dim dawn of an eternal day. And in the light of those bright worlds and of that dawning Day they press securely forward, borne on their way by the breath of heaven across the trackless waters of time towards, and in full view of, the haven of eternal rest.

NOTES.

I

THE ORIGIN OF THE MORAL SENSE.

NOT a few modern writers have endeavoured to account for the Moral Sense as an inherited belief evoked and fostered by man's felt dependence on his fellows and by the manifest benefit to the race of virtue and the manifestly injurious tendency of vice. This theory is stated in chapters iv. and v. of Darwin's *Descent of Man.* Similarly Spencer says on page 123 of his *Data of Ethics*, quoting a letter from himself to J. S. Mill:[1] "To make my position fully understood, it seems needful to add that, corresponding to the fundamental propositions of a developed Moral Science, there have been, and still are, developing in the race, certain fundamental moral intuitions; and that, though these moral intuitions are the results of accumulated experiences of utility, gradually organized and inherited, they have come to be quite independent of conscious experience. . . . I believe that the experiences of utility organized and consolidated through all past generations of the human race, have been producing corresponding nervous modifications, which, by continual transmission and accumulation, have become in us certain faculties of moral intuition—certain emotions responding

---

Quoted at greater length on p. 721 of Bain's *Mental and Moral Science.*

to right and wrong conduct, which have no apparent basis in the individual experiences of utility." This theory has been well called Evolutionary Ethics. It has been accepted by almost all teachers belonging to the modern school of Scientific Agnosticism.[1]

It may be at once admitted that the moral sense is strengthened immensely by our observation day by day that what we call virtue and vice tend respectively to the benefit and the injury of the race; and that this observation frequently moulds our judgment of the conduct of ourselves and others. For the manifest tendency of right and wrong action reveals the harmony between the Supreme Judge within and the constitution of human life and of human society. And this observed harmony increases the authority of the Voice within.

But this explanation fails utterly to explain the most important elements of the case. It does nothing whatever to account for the unique and peremptory and indisputable authority of the Moral Sense. This authority is manifestly independent of mere utility. For we are frequently compelled to pay highest honour to a man who dares to do right at the risk or cost even of life. On the other hand, we ever condemn and despise the man whose conduct is determined only by its probable results. These judgments cannot be accounted for by the observed utility of virtue and the evil effects of vice.

That virtue benefits and vice injures, is in complete agreement with the Christian hypothesis of this lecture. For if man and the moral sense were made and are ruled by a Supreme Intelligence, and if the moral sense is His

[1] See Note iii.

Will inwoven into the nature of man, we wonder not that the law written within is for man's highest good. And, as already said, this observed tendency helps to develop the inborn moral sense. The opinion now combated is that the moral sense is completely explained by the past and present needs and surroundings of human life.

This theory lies open to a still more serious objection. If the moral sense is only a heritage accumulated by long observation of the effect of right and wrong doing, it has no intrinsic authority; and man is left without any adequate motive for choosing ever the right and resisting under all circumstances the wrong. The ordinary general effects of virtue and vice are far from being a motive sufficient in all cases. For not unfrequently we think ourselves quite able to escape all evil consequences of sin. Sometimes it seems as though our sin would do no harm to ourselves or to others. And, even when our sin is likely to injure others, we may ask, Why should I sacrifice my pleasure to another's profit? To this question, the theory before us has no answer to give. The moral teaching of Christ, as of Buddha and of Mohammed, gives a complete answer to it by pointing to inevitable and absolute recompense beyond the grave.

This lack of a universally applicable motive for right doing is a fatal objection to the theory before us. For in the moral conflict of life every one needs to be armed with decisive reasons for resisting all inducements to evil. The doctrine we are considering leaves us in that conflict without any protection whatever against the many solicitations to sin. In other words, this professedly moral teaching fails utterly to supply man's pressing moral need. Nay more. It breaks down all barriers against immorality. For if it be, as it claims to be, a statement of the whole case, there is no reason whatever why we should not enjoy the pleasures of sin if we can only escape its consequences. Better far to believe in Buddhist transmigration than in such a doctrine as this.

Some will object that reward and punishment are poor motives for virtue. But that they are effective, all human government bears witness. It is an immense gain to morality to have a lower motive, appreciated by all, to fall back upon when higher motives fail. Such lower motive is always needful. Whatever breaks it down undermines the stability of the social fabric.

Fortunately the injurious tendency of this teaching proves it to be untrue. For, being manifestly fatal to man's highest interests, even if true it would be better for us not to know it, better to believe what in that case would be the erroneous teaching of Jesus of Nazareth. In other words —to repeat an argument already used—in that case, ignorance would be better than knowledge, error better than truth. This cannot be. We therefore need not hesitate to reject as untrue that which we have found, by repeated experience, to be morally injurious.

The practical tendency of this teaching becomes very evident in the following quotation. On page 93 of his *Data of Ethics*, Spencer says: "The broken leg which a drunkard's accident causes, counts among those miseries brought on self and family by intemperance, which form the ground for reprobating it; but if anxiety to fulfil duties prompts the continued use of a sprained knee spite of the pain, and brings on a chronic lameness involving lack of exercise, consequent ill-health, inefficiency, anxiety, and unhappiness, it is supposed that ethics has no verdict to give in the matter. A student who is plucked because he has spent in amusement the time and money that should have gone in study, is blamed for thus making parents unhappy and preparing for himself a miserable future; but another who, thinking exclusively of claims on him, reads night after night with hot or aching head, and, breaking down, cannot take his degree, but returns home shattered in health and unable to support himself, is named with pity only, as not subject to any moral judgment; or rather the moral judgment passed in wholly favourable."

A writer who cannot see the infinite difference between the "miseries brought on self and family by intemperance" and the "chronic lameness" caused by "anxiety to fulfil duties" is, as lacking the simplest Data of Ethics, beyond reach of argument in matters of morals. But he may serve as a warning of the tendency of the school he represents.

On the subject of this note, I recommend very strongly the chapter on *Hedonism with Evolution* in vol. ii. of Martineau's *Types of Ethical Theory*. An exceedingly good popular discussion of the same is found in Section iii. of Davison's *Christian Conscience*.

II.

FREEDOM OR NECESSITY.

J. S. Mill, in bk. vi. ch. 2 of his *System of Logic*, writes as follows:—"The question, whether the law of causality applies in the same strict sense to human actions as to other phenomena, is the celebrated controversy concerning the freedom of the will: which from at least as far back as the time of Pelagius, has divided both the philosophical and the religious world. The affirmative opinion is commonly called the doctrine of Necessity, as asserting human volitions and actions to be necessary and inevitable. The negative maintains that the will is not determined, like other phenomena, by antecedents, but determines itself; that our volitions are not, properly speaking, the effects of causes, or at least have no causes which they uniformly and implicitly obey.

"I have already made it sufficiently apparent that the former of these opinions is that which I consider the true one; but the misleading terms in which it is often expressed, and the indistinct manner in which it is usually apprehended, have both obstructed its reception, and perverted its influence when received. The metaphysical theory of free-will, as held by philosophers, (for the practical feeling of it, common in a greater or less degree to all mankind, is in no way inconsistent with the contrary theory,) was invented because the supposed alternative of admitting human actions to be *necessary*, was deemed inconsistent with every one's instinctive consciousness, as well as humiliating to the pride and even degrading to the moral nature of man. Nor do I deny that the doctrine as sometimes held, is open to these imputations; for the misapprehension in which I shall be able to show that they originate, unfortunately is not confined to the opponents of the doctrine, but is participated in by many, perhaps we might say by most, of its supporters.

"Correctly conceived, the doctrine called Philosophical

Necessity is simply this : that, given the motives which are present to an individual's mind, and given likewise the character and disposition of the individual, the manner in which he will act might be unerringly inferred: that if we knew the person thoroughly, and knew all the inducements which are acting upon him, we could foretell his conduct with as much certainty as we can predict any physical event."

We have similar teaching in a chapter on *Liberty and Necessity* in Bain's work on *The Emotions and the Will*, and in another chapter on the same subject in his work on *Mental and Moral Science*.

Similarly again Spencer, in a chapter on *The Will* in his *Principles of Psychology*, speaks of man's sense of freedom as an "illusion" which "consists in supposing that at each moment the ego is something more than the aggregate of feelings and ideas, actual and nascent, which then exists." This illusion, he declares to be strengthened by " the extreme complication of the forces" producing human volitions. The doctrine of Necessity as understood by Mill is universally accepted by all modern Agnostics as a logical result of their principles.

Let us see what this doctrine involves. If every action could be predicted with certainty, were its antecedents known, it must be an invariable consequence of its antecedents, or in other words an inevitable outworking of irresistible forces. The appearance of compulsion, the above writers guard against by teaching that inclination and volition are the antecedents of action, as they are the consequents of other antecedents.

These forces or antecedents, we may divide into three

classes, viz. man's formed disposition, his bodily and mental constitution received at birth, and various external influences. The second class is, however, merged in the third. For the constitution received at birth is a consequence of conditions earlier than, and therefore external to, the newly-born one. Indeed, if every action and every volition is an outworking of irresistible forces, man's formed character, inasmuch as it is formed by successive volitions and actions, must be itself an inevitable result of forces operating either during his lifetime or before his birth. In other words, on this theory, man is, in every sense, a creature of circumstances and antecedents.

If this be so, man is, even in the moment of decision and action, not active but absolutely passive. He is no more the author of his own actions than is a pen the cause of a letter written with it. He is only the arena of a conflict of motives, or at most the umpire who impartially measures their strength and awards to the strongest the prerogative of decision.

This theory fails utterly to account for the facts of the case, especially for man's deep conviction that in action he is not passive but active, that in the conflict of motives the decision is with himself, and with himself alone. Upon this assumption rests every estimate of man about himself and others. A conviction so deep and so widespread cannot be an illusion. Certainly we cannot accept without clear and strong proof so unlikely a suggestion.

The proofs of this theory, its advocates are not very eager to produce. For the more part they assume it to be true, and content themselves with clearing away misconceptions or replying to sundry objections. Or, if closely pressed, they would probably say that it is a logical inference from the necessary assumption that every phenomenon is an invariable consequence of definite antecedents, known or unknown, seen or unseen; or in other words that for every effect there is an adequate cause. And it must be admitted that the advance of science has in a multitude of cases discovered invariable antecedents where previously none were thought to exist. But we have no proof that the chain of effect and cause goes back for ever. Indeed, this is inconceivable. And, if not, we must at last, tracing up the chain of causation, come to a cause which has no cause external to itself. We thus reach an ultimate cause.

Already we have seen that man's immoveable conviction that in action he might have acted otherwise than he did, his condemnation of himself and others for wrong action, and the moral healthfulness of that condemnation, are strong evidence that his actions have their ultimate source in himself. We have now seen that we have no reason to deny that phenomena have ultimate causes. And if so, we have nothing to set against the strong evidence just quoted that man is himself the ultimate cause of his own actions. This by no means implies that man's actions are effects without causes, but that their cause lies hidden in the mystery of human personality. Just so, the ultimate cause of the universe lies hid in the personal Will and Nature of God.

We must therefore admit in human action an all-important factor other than those mentioned above, viz. the man himself. The accidents of our birth and training and circumstances tend to mould our disposition and our action. But upon ourselves it depends whether, and how far, we yield to these tendencies, and how far they actually mould us. The ultimate decision can be traced no further than ourselves: and there in each case it remains, to our honour or to our shame.

On this whole subject I recommend strongly the chapter on *Determinism and Free Will* in vol. ii. of Martineau's *Study of Religion*.

The least satisfactory part of Dr. Martineau's treatment of this subject is, in my view, his attempt to harmonize God's prescience with man's freedom by assuming a "self-limitation" of divine foresight. He seems to me to confound contingency with uncertainty. A better reconciliation is that mere knowledge exerts no influence on the object known, any more than mere vision on an object seen. If so, mere foresight exerts no influence on the object or event foreseen, and is in no way inconsistent with contingency. Consequently, our belief in an infinite and eternal Intelligence by no means excludes the possibility of free agents. We may conceive God to create free agents, and these making free choice under the contemplation of His eternal foresight.

III.

Scientific Agnosticism.

The modern writers quoted in Section iii. may be conveniently grouped together as representing Scientific Agnosticism. The title Agnostic was chosen, as he tells us in the *Nineteenth Century* for February 1889, by Professor Huxley, to describe the position of some who disclaim any assured knowledge of an intelligent Creator or of life beyond the grave, or think such knowledge unattainable. The specific term Scientific Agnosticism, I have used to describe a group of men conspicuous as teachers of Natural Science and holding certain definite scientific opinions.

Already on page 19 we have found Darwin admitting his inability to arrive at assured conviction about the existence of God. In his *Life and Letters*, vol. i. p. 304, we find him writing: "In my most extreme fluctuations I have never been an Atheist in the sense of denying the existence of God. I think generally (and more and more as I grow older), but not always, that an Agnostic would be the more correct description of my state of mind." Again, on page 307: "For myself I do not believe that there ever has been any revelation. As for a future life, every man must judge for himself between conflicting and vague probabilities." And on page 312 f.: "When thus reflecting I feel compelled to look to a First Cause having an intelligent mind in some degree analogous to that of man; and I deserve to be called a Theist. This conclusion was strong in my mind about the time, as far as I can remember, when I wrote the *Origin of Species*; and it is since that time that it has very gradually, with many fluctuations, become weaker. But then arises the doubt, can the mind of man, which has, as I fully believe, been developed from a mind as low as that possessed by the lowest animals, be trusted when it draws such grand conclusions?

"I cannot pretend to throw the least light on such abstruse problems. The mystery of the beginning of all things is insoluble by us; and I for one must be content to remain an Agnostic."

This last quotation shows how Darwin's own self-respect was lowered by his oversight of the essential and infinite difference between men and animals; an oversight implied in his theory that the mind of man was evolved, by the outworking of natural forces, from the instinct of animals. This oversight is common to the entire school of thought now before us.

Darwin endeavours to account for the variety of living forms and especially for the higher forms of life by the operation of influences now at work wherever there is life, especially by the many variations of offspring from their parents, by the survival of useful variations, and by the transmission of these variations to descendants. This he suitably describes as Natural Selection, or the Survival of the Fittest in the struggle for existence. He endeavours to account by this theory of Evolution for the growth of the moral sense; but refuses to discuss the origin of life.

Herbert Spencer [1] agrees with Darwin in accepting, and giving great importance to, the above theory of Evolution; but differs from him in making Evolution the keystone of a System of Philosophy in which he endeavours to account for all the phenomena of the universe by the unvarying operation of forces at work in inorganic matter before the dawn of life. These principles he advocated before the appearance, in A.D. 1859, of Darwin's *Origin of Species*.

Spencer speaks of the "First Cause" as "Unknowable." Yet in his *First Principles*, sec. 27, he says: "Though the Absolute cannot in any manner or degree be known, in the strict sense of knowing, yet we find that its positive existence is a necessary datum of consciousness; and so

[1] See especially his *Factors of Organic Evolution*.

long as consciousness continues, we cannot for an instant rid it of this datum; and that thus the belief which this datum constitutes, has a higher warrant than any other whatever." Similarly, in sec. 31, he says: "The certainty that on the one hand such a Power exists, while on the other hand its nature transcends intuition and is beyond imagination, is the certainty towards which intelligence has from the first been progressing. To this conclusion Science inevitably arrives as it reaches its confines; while to this conclusion Religion is irresistibly driven by criticism. And satisfying as it does the demands of the most rigorous logic at the same time that it gives the religious sentiment the widest possible sphere of action, it is the conclusion we are bound to accept without reserve or qualification."

To speak of God as Unknowable, while writing thus about the Ultimate Cause, is to give to the word *knowledge* a very loose meaning. By knowledge, "in the strict sense of knowing," I understand assurance of that which is true, for sufficient reasons. Such an assurance indisputably is Mr. Spencer's certainty that there exists an " Ultimate Cause."

He may, however, in spite of this knowledge, be suitably described as an Agnostic. For he denies any further knowledge of God except that He is "an Inscrutable Power." Indeed, he endeavours to show the "impiety" of forming any conception of God other than this; and illustrates the "presumption of theologians" in so doing by comparing them to a watch assuming that its maker's actions were "determined, like its own, by springs and escapements." But a conscious and intelligent watch might fairly assume, in view of its own capacity for orderly and useful movement, that its maker was superior to itself. And this is all that any intelligent theologian professes to know about God. If there be an Ultimate Cause, it is reasonable to infer with certainty that whatever in man is great and good has a greater and better counterpart in Him. Inasmuch then as we use the word *person* to describe that which distinguishes man from animals, we need not hesitate, in spite of this charge of impiety, to attribute personality to the "Ultimate Cause." To this extent, and even further than this, man may know God.

While professing ignorance of all that which to the Christian is most worth knowing, Spencer endeavours, and with very great ability, to sketch the past history and the future destiny of the universe. He tries to show that whatever exists or has taken place in matter, or in action, or in thought, is an outworking of forces operating in or on matter from the earliest formation of our planet to the present time; that these forces acting invariably according to their own laws produced out of homogeneity variety, out of lifelessness life and intelligence and moral sense and the whole drama of human history; and that the same forces by their continued working will produce universal death and dissolution and equilibrium and return to homogeneity. But he recoils from the thought that eternal quiescence is the ultimate fate of the universe; and therefore timidly suggests that possibly, (as a pendulum having reached its limit returns, so) the continued operation of the forces which have produced universal dissolution may in turn reproduce movement and life.

This last point may be illustrated by a quotation from *First Principles*, sec. 183. "Motion as well as Matter being fixed in quantity, it would seem that the change in the distribution of Matter which Motion effects, coming to a limit in whichever direction it is carried, the indestructible Motion thereupon necessitates a reverse distribution. Apparently, the universally coexistent forces of attraction and repulsion, which, as we have seen, necessitate rhythm in all minor changes throughout the Universe, also necessitate rhythm in the totality of its changes—produce now an immeasurable period during which the attractive forces predominating cause universal concentration, and then an immeasurable period during which the repulsive forces predominating, cause universal diffusion—alternate eras of Evolution and Dissolution. And thus there is suggested the conception of a past during which there have been successive Evolutions analogous to that which is now going on; and a future during which successive other such Evolutions may go on—ever the same in principle but never the same in concrete result."

In other words, life is related to matter as foam to the ocean, except that its forms are many and various and their evolution gradual. It is the temporary form assumed by matter under the operation of forces operating wherever there is matter. Spencer's whole series of *Synthetic Philosophy* is a skilful and elaborate attempt to expound and justify this conception of the universe. He is appropriately named by Agnostics,[1] "Our Great Philosopher."

A theory differing from the above in many details, yet practically the same, has been propounded with great confidence by Professor Haeckel of Jena. The assumption which underlies it is stated plainly at the beginning of his

---

[1] Darwin, *Descent of Man*, p. 123; Haeckel, *History of Creation*, vol. ii. p. 367.

most popular work. In his *History of Creation*, vol. i. p. 20, we read as follows: "Whilst, then, we emphatically oppose the vital or teleological view of animate nature which presents animal and vegetable forms as the productions of a kind Creator, acting for a definite purpose, or of a creative, natural force acting for a definite purpose, we must, on the other hand, decidedly adopt that view of the universe which is called the *mechanical* or *causal*. It may also be called the *monistic*, or *single-principle* theory, as opposed to the *two-fold principle*, or *dualistic* theory, which is necessarily implied in the teleological conception of the universe. The mechanical view of nature has for many years been so firmly established in certain domains of natural science, that it is here unnecessary to say much about it. It no longer occurs to physicists, chemists, mineralogists, or astronomers, to seek to find in the phenomena which continually appear before them in their scientific domain the action of a Creator acting for a definite purpose. They universally, and without hesitation, look upon the phenomena which appear in their different departments of study as the necessary and invariable effects of physical and chemical forces which are inherent in matter. Thus far their view is purely *materialistic*, in a certain sense of that word of many meanings."

On page 35 he continues: "Scientific materialism, which is identical with our Monism, affirms in reality no more than that everything in the world goes on naturally—that every effect has its cause, and every cause its effect. It therefore assigns to causal law—that is, the law of a necessary connexion between cause and effect—its place over the entire series of phenomena that can be known. At the same time, scientific materialism positively rejects every belief in the miraculous, and every conception, in whatever form it appears, of supernatural processes. Accordingly, nowhere in the whole domain of human knowledge does it recognise real metaphysics, but throughout only physics; through it the inseparable connexion between matter, form, and force becomes self-evident. This scientific materialism has long since been so universally acknowledged in the wide domain of inorganic science, in Physics and Chemistry, in Mineralogy and Geology, that no one now doubts its sole authority. But in Biology, or Organic Science, the case is very different; here its value is still continually a matter of dispute in many quarters. There is, however, nothing else that can be set up against it, excepting the metaphysical spectre of a vital power, or empty theological dogma. If we can prove that all nature, so far as it can be known, is only *one*, that the same 'great, eternal, iron laws' are active in the life of animals and plants, as in the growth of crystals and in the force of steam, we may with reason maintain the monistic or mechanical view of things throughout the domain of Biology—in Zoology and Botany—whether it be stigmatized as 'materialism' or not. In such a sense all exact science, and the law of cause and effect at its head, is purely materialistic."

So on page 37: "This principle is quite inseparable from our Non-miraculous History of Creation, and characterizes it as opposed to the teleological belief in the miracles of a Supernatural History of Creation." With this principle, as we saw on page 66, the writer does not hesitate to say that everything must be made to fit. Haeckel traces on a map the migrations of our race from its original home in a continent now covered by the Indian Ocean to the ends of the earth; and with ingenuity and complete confidence traces up the pedigree of man through apes, kangaroos, frogs, and worms, to the simplest forms of life. Like some other Agnostics he possesses the gift of prophecy; and appropriately closes the work before us with a glowing prediction. "Just as this new monistic philosophy first opens up to us a true understanding of the real universe, so its application to practical human life must open up a new road towards moral perfection. By its aid we shall at last begin to raise ourselves out of the state of social barbarism in which, notwithstanding the much-vaunted civilisation of our century, we are still plunged. . . . Future centuries will celebrate our age, which was occupied with laying the foundations of the Doctrine of Descent, as the new era in which began a period of human development, rich in blessings,—a period which was characterized by the victory of free inquiry over the despotism of authority, and by the powerful ennobling influence of the Monistic Philosophy."

Haeckel's theory of the universe is reproduced with Haeckel's confidence, and the main facts of modern science are clearly and comprehensively and I believe on the whole correctly stated by Edward Clodd in an attractive volume on *The Story of Creation*. He differs from his predecessors in limiting the word *force* to influences tending to bring together masses and molecules and atoms, such as gravitation and chemical affinity; and the word *energy* to influences tending to separate masses or molecules, such as heat and an electric current. Force and Energy he groups together as two forms of *Power*. This distinction seems to me real and important. But, by giving a new limitation to familiar words, *e.g.* to Spencer's well-known phrase *Persistence of Force*, which he uses as equivalent to, whereas Clodd distinguishes it from, *Conservation of Energy*, his language is sometimes confusing.

Clodd covers, and with great skill, in one small volume the ground occupied by Spencer's voluminous works. After discussing the evolution of the Universe, of Life, of Life-forms, and of Species, he goes on to expound the "Evolution of Mind, Society, Language, Art, and Science, Morals, Theology." All these are, in his view, an outworking of forces operating invariably in or upon matter, according to their own laws, long before life began, and operating to the present hour. The following quotation from page 206 explains his position :—

"*Evolution of Mind.*—If the theory of evolution be not universal, the germs of decay are in it. And here we pass from what is interesting to what is of serious import for us, because if the phenomena of mind are not capable of the like mechanical explanation as the phenomena of stars and planets, and of vegetable and animal life, evolution remains only a speculation to fascinate the curious. It can, in that case, furnish no rule of life or motive to conduct, and man, 'the roof and crown of things,' would be the sole witness against their unity and totality. If there be in him any faculty which is no part of the contents of the universe, if there be anything done by him which lies outside the range of causation, then the doctrine of the Conservation of Energy falls to pieces, for man has the power to add to that which the physicist demonstrates can neither be increased nor lessened."

Our author concludes his work by saying: "All that it

really suffices us to learn for the discharge of life's duties, and all the motive that is needed to impel us thereto, is supplied in the theory which has so profoundly and permanently affected every department of human thought."

In other words, the new theory is everything or nothing. Either it explains everything which is or has been in matter or mind, or it is not true. At least, this is the only meaning I can attach to the phrase, "the germs of decay are in it." And if true, it is all we need to know. These stupendous claims, which are practically the same as those advanced by Spencer and Haeckel for the same theory, we will test for a moment in the light of the evidence before us.

Already in Section iii. we have seen that the known forces now at work in the material world do nothing whatever to explain the origin of life. This subject Spencer omits from his original prospectus, "partly because, even without it, the scheme is too extensive; and partly because the interpretation of Organic Nature after the proposed method, is of more immediate importance." He thus omits an essential link of the chain of his *Synthetic Philosophy*. This omission he acknowledges and scantily supplies by a letter to an American Review which is appended to vol. i. of his *Principles of Biology*. He there explains how an organic compound (others might have been added) has been produced by the manipulation of chemists in the laboratory. But this no more proves that natural forces are able to produce such combinations than that they are able to produce a work of art. It still remains that these complex combinations are never found except where there is or has been life.

Organic forms, Spencer accounts for by supposing that in these forms the molecules of organic matter, acted upon by their environment and guided by their own polarities, find equilibrium. The only illustration of this suggestion which he quotes is the crystal. And we have already seen [1] that in essential points crystals differ from living bodies.

Haeckel's attempt to explain the origin of life has been already discussed.[2]

In a short chapter devoted to the same subject, Clodd contents himself with saying on page 150 that "The Origin of life is not a more stupendous problem to solve than the origin of water;" and that "It does not seem after all such a far cry from the crystal to the amœba as from the amœba to Plato and Newton." But we have no shadow of proof that the gulf between the amœba and Newton has been spanned by the operation of natural forces. Moreover, the very mysterious transition of gases into water is taking place daily before our eyes, thus revealing the operation now of a force competent to produce it. The transition from the lifeless to the living has never been observed. And the unbridged chasm remains a silent but decisive witness to the operation in time gone by of a force altogether different from, and higher than, the forces observed in operation now.

Already in Note i. we have seen that the theory before us fails utterly to explain the unique and supremely important distinction of right and wrong, a distinction as wide as human literature and as human thought and life; and that it fails to supply man's urgent moral need for a

---

[1] See page 56.   [2] See page 63.

universally applicable and strong motive for right doing and breaks down the most powerful motives which in the past have aided man's moral life. In Note ii. we have seen that this theory contradicts the deep and universal and morally most helpful conviction of man that in choice of action he is not passive but active, himself the supreme arbiter of his own action.

On page 52 we have seen that this theory leaves unexplained the vast difference between animals and man. Indeed, the whole tendency of the school before us is to minimise this difference.

Once more and most conspicuously, the theory we are discussing fails to account for the unique position of Christianity among the religions of the world. Its advocates speak much about the evolution of morals and of society, and hold out great hopes of the more rapid progress which would follow the acceptance of their principles. How comes it then that this evolution takes place, and during many centuries has taken place, only in those nations which recognise the Carpenter of Nazareth as infinitely the greatest of men?[1] This all-important question, like that of the origin of life, Spencer leaves unnoticed in his *Synthetic Philosophy*. Either he has no answer to give, or the important facts which prompt this question have not attracted his attention.[2]

---

[1] See Section iv.

[2] This omission is specially conspicuous in the volume on *Ecclesiastical Institutions*, where Spencer endeavours to show that all forms of religious life are an outworking of natural forces. He points out various elements common to Christianity and other religions; and appeals to these as proofs of common origin. But of the unique superiority of Christianity he is quite unconscious.

These facts, incapable of explanation by it, prove that the theory before us is not, as it claims to be, a complete theory of the universe. It is not "completely unified knowledge." The unexplained facts reveal the operation of forces other than those which this theory recognises. We must seek for a theory embracing both the facts of Natural Science and these other facts. Such a theory, the Christian theory, I have in this lecture endeavoured to trace.

On the other hand, the failure of the theory of Evolution to explain all phenomena, by no means proves that "the germs of decay are in it;"[1] whatever these words mean. The theory of Gravitation does not explain chemical and vital phenomena. Yet it is true; and, in its own sphere, universal. Chemical and vital forces all acknowledge the sway of gravitation. Living bodies fall as quickly as do lifeless ones. So do bodies in which rapid chemical reaction is taking place. It seems to me that the theory we are discussing, viz. that existing forms are products of unvarying forces acting according to their own laws, is a generalisation of great value and of wide and perhaps universal validity. No one doubts that the stratified rocks were deposited by the operation of forces still at work in various parts of the surface of the earth, of forces operating before the earliest stratified rocks were formed. All admit that both plants and animals have been modified in their descent from generation to generation. And, if so, it is not easy to fix limits to such modification. Evidently, cognate languages have been evolved, under influence of environment, from a common stock. And we need not

[1] See page 173.

deny that the outward forms of the Christian life have been so evolved. All I contend for is that this important principle will not account for all the known facts of the case.

It is at once evident that the theories about the origin of the moral sense and about the causation of human action, discussed in Notes i. and ii., are involved in, though they by no means involve, the theories of Spencer and Haeckel. Indeed, these last are but an extension of Mill's theory of causation, in the light of scientific observation, to account for the manifold forms of vegetable and animal life.

From the above quotations it appears that under guise of a title modestly professing ignorance our Scientific Agnostics claim to know everything, or at least everything man needs to know.

In concluding this criticism, I cannot refrain from acknowledging the wide knowledge and great ability of those whose opinions I have been compelled to condemn; and the great services they have rendered to the advancement of human thought. Indeed, the accuracy of their methods of investigation has taught a much-needed lesson to students of Ethics and of Theology. Especially to Herbert Spencer are these acknowledgments due. Among his many works I may mention his *Principles of Biology* as having been very helpful to me. He has taught us, more fully than any earlier teacher, that the Universe and Life are one, permeated by the same or similar forces and governed by the same or similar laws. Yet I cannot cast off a conviction that with truth so important is mingled error destructive not only of religion but of morality. He has erred, it seems to me, by failing to observe the limits of his own, in great part correct, generalisations. By mistaking a partial truth for the whole truth, he has fallen I think into serious error.

Similar recognition is due to Darwin's abundant and careful collections of facts and to his thoughtful and modest inferences from them. I notice that he refuses to make his inductions the basis of a theory of the Universe; and acknowledges at the close of his *Origin of Species* that they are in harmony with belief in a Creator. Darwin thus differs widely from the other writers here mentioned.

As a very able criticism of the theory discussed in this note, I am glad to recommend W. Arthur's volume on *Agnosticism and Mr. Herbert Spencer.*

IV.

THE BIBLE AND SCIENCE.

The argument of this lecture has not assumed, or attempted to prove, the infallible authority of Holy Scripture. Yet, apart from such assumption or proof, we have found in the Christian documents, testing these as we should any other ancient writings and reading them in the light of the effect of Christianity upon the world, complete proof that Christ taught certain doctrines, made for Himself certain claims, and in proof of them rose from the dead. This argument would remain valid even if it were proved that some of the statements of the Bible contradict assured results of natural science. For, although, if as we have endeavoured to prove God gave His Eternal Son to live on earth and teach and die and rise again in order to save the world, it is reasonable to expect that He would secure for men a sufficient and correct record of the words and works of Christ—for without such record these would benefit only His immediate hearers—we have no reason to expect that this record would contain anticipations of the discoveries of modern science; and, if not, its writers could hardly avoid using here and there forms of speech contradicting these later discoveries.

There are, however, remarkable points of contact between the old story of Genesis and the older story of the rocks which claim from us, even in connexion with this lecture, a moment's attention. We shall notice in order points of agreement, points of difference, and points in which comparison fails through silence of one or other of the witnesses.

The Book of Genesis anticipates recent discovery by saying that the world was not always as it is now, that our planet is older than the oldest life upon it, that irrational animals are older than man, that the earliest animals lived in water, and that these were followed by birds and mammals.[1] In both records we read that the various forms of life did not arise together and were not coeval with the earth, but that higher forms were preceded by lower ones.

Another remarkable coincidence is the mention of *great sea-monsters* (R.V.) in Gen. i. 21. The word so rendered denotes in Deut. xxxii. 33 (A.V. and R.V. *dragon*) a

[1] The earliest remains of mammals are older than the earliest assured remains of birds. But, indisputably, birds are nearer kin to reptiles than to mammals. And the absence of very early remains of birds, whose wings would save them from many modes of death which preserved the forms of other animals, is small proof that they were not actually earlier than mammals.

poisonous serpent. But it denotes usually a dweller in the water, and in Isa. xxvii. 1, li. 9, apparently the Egyptian crocodile. No Hebrew word could more suitably describe the great water saurians which were so conspicuous a feature of the Secondary strata long before mammals became prevalent.

Even the mention in Genesis of plants before animals is not without scientific significance. For indisputably, although the distinction between them vanishes in their lower forms, vegetables are lower than animals, and are in some sense intermediate between inorganic bodies and animals.

To the above coincidences may be added the scientific probability that when first aqueous vapour was condensed, water enveloped the entire globe.

Similar teaching, but less definite, is found in the Sacred Books of other nations. As an example I may quote the Hindu *Rig-Veda*, Mandala x. 129:[1]

> " In the beginning there was neither nought nor aught,
> Then there was neither sky nor atmosphere above.
> What then enshrouded all this teeming Universe?
> In the receptacle of what was it contained?
> Was it enveloped in the gulf profound of water?
> Then there was neither death nor immortality,
> Then was there neither day, nor night, nor light, nor darkness.
> Only the Existent One breathed calmly, self-contained.
> Nought else than him there was—nought else above, beyond.
> Then first came darkness hid in darkness, gloom in gloom.
> Next all was water, all a chaos indiscreet,
> In which the One lay void, shrouded in nothingness.
> Then turning inwards he by self-developed force
> Of inner fervour and intense abstraction, grew.

---

[1] From Monier Williams' *Hindu Wisdom*, p. 22. It is practically the same as the rendering given in H. H. Wilson's translation of the *Rig-Veda-Sarhita*.

> And now in him Desire, the primal germ of mind,
> Arose, which learned men, profoundly searching, say
> Is the first subtle bond, connecting Entity
> With Nullity. This ray that kindled dormant life,
> Where was it then ? before ? or was it found above ?
> Were there parturient powers and latent qualities,
> And fecund principles beneath, and active forces
> That energized aloft ? Who knows ? Who can declare ?
> How and from what has sprung this Universe ? the gods
> Themselves are subsequent to its development.
> Who, then, can penetrate the secret of its rise ?
> Whether 'twas framed or not, made or not made ; he only
> Who in the highest heaven sits, the omniscient lord,
> Assuredly knows all, or haply knows he not."

The knowledge of God revealed in the above beautiful quotation is in complete harmony with the teaching of Paul in Rom. i. 19, 20. Its tone of uncertainty is in harmony with the less favoured position, if the Gospel be true, of the other nations as compared with the chosen race. It is also right to say that the hymn quoted above from the *Rig-Veda* is preceded and followed by others containing only empty ritual; whereas in Genesis the story of the creation is followed by a consecutive narrative in which the Creator of the World draws near to man as the God of Abraham and Isaac and Jacob. This makes an infinite practical difference between the two books. And it warns us that selections from an unknown work may give a very wrong conception of the work as a whole.

The coincidence noted above is much more important than at first sight appears. For it shows us that long before the earliest investigation of the crust of the earth men knew that the beautiful world around them was once an empty waste, and that the various forms of animals and then man successively appeared upon it. How came they thus to anticipate these remarkable results of science ?

Their early knowledge of matters completely beyond their observation seems to me to bear witness to a divine revelation.

In view of these points of agreement, the apparent contradictions sink into insignificance. That land insects are first mentioned on the sixth day along with the mammals, need not surprise us. For, taken as wholes, the inhabitants of the water were earlier than those of the dry land.

A more serious objection is that fruit-trees are placed earlier than the sun. This may perhaps be partly explained by the two corresponding triplets in which the six days are arranged. The heavenly bodies may suitably be represented as inhabitants of the light created on the first day; as were fishes and birds of the sea and atmosphere prepared for them on the second day, and mammals and man of the dry land brought to light on the third day. Moreover, although it is all-important for us to know that the sun and moon and stars, so potent in the thought of the ancient world, were made by Him who made man and who afterwards revealed Himself to Abraham, at Sinai, and in Christ, the order of time of their creation has no spiritual significance whatever.

Possibly there is a deeper reason for the late place given in the six days' work to the creation of the heavenly bodies.

We have been told with triumph by Haeckel[1] and others that our earth has been dethroned from its unique place of honour as the supposed centre of the universe and compelled to occupy a subordinate place as a mere satellite to one among many other greater bodies, or

[1] *History of Creation*, vol. ii. p. 264.

rather as an atom of dust lost in the vastness of infinite space.

The relative importance of the earth as compared with other heavenly bodies depends upon whether or not these last are inhabited by rational beings. For, certainly bulk is no measure of importance. The animated matter of our globe is infinitesimal as compared with the inanimate, yet of infinitely greater importance. It seems to me quite possible that in the entire material universe our small planet is the only home of life. That the larger planets are inhabited, is very unlikely: and even Venus and Mars seem to be much less favourable to life than is our earth. Already we have seen that life cannot be accounted for by the operation of the forces at work in inorganic matter. It must therefore, wherever found, be an outworking of a higher power. Moreover, apart from inhabitants in them, the existence of the heavenly bodies may easily be explained. For, if creation be the accomplishment of a divine purpose, the instruction of man would be a sufficient motive for the creation of the stars. They are a stupendous mirror in which we see reflected the greatness of the Creator. Their size, their distances, their movements, make visible in some sense the infinity and even the eternity of God. Without them, our race would be infinitely poorer. If, as the Gospel asserts, the Creator paid to our planet the unique honour of becoming one of its inhabitants, we need not be surprised to learn that He had already surrounded with the wondrous panorama of the visible heavens the future home of those whom He afterwards came to save. Even the subordinate place of our earth as dependent upon the sun for light and heat is in remarkable harmony with the dependent position of the race living upon it. Certainly the relation of our planet to the stellar universe presents nothing inconsistent with the Gospel of Christ.

In the above sense we may think of the sun, moon, and stars as subordinate to man. Certainly they were made by our Father for our delight and instruction, and in order to shed light on our path and guide our steps; and the sun was made to ripen our harvests and give us food. This subordinate purpose receives its meet expression in the story of creation by the mention of the heavenly bodies as created not before, but after, the planetary home of man.

We find then between the story of Genesis and the story of the rocks important coincidences. Some of these, especially that the world was not always an abode of life, are as we saw in Section iii. of considerable theological importance. The points of apparent contradiction are of no spiritual significance whatever; and are such as a religious teacher writing for the masses would, even if he knew them, naturally omit.

A greater difference remains to be noticed. The rocks are silent about certain matters touching most closely the highest interests of all men. They say nothing about the origin of man and of those tremendous natural forces which sometimes threaten to crush him. The eye of science, with vision at last made clear, has been able to contemplate the evolution of order out of chaos, and out of lifelessness life in its successively higher forms until it reached its crown in man. But it has no ears to hear the voice of Him who summoned order and life out of chaos and lifelessness; and is thus unable to appreciate the intelligent purpose to which that voice gave utterance.

This more important lesson is taught, in a form which all can understand, in one of the oldest books in the world.

If any one thinks that Genesis is disproved by modern science, or needs to be corrected by it, let him try to compose a story of creation better fitted for the needs of mankind than the record which has come down to us from the early morning of human literature.

The elementary truths of religion, which were needed at once by all men everywhere, were revealed in the childhood of our race: other truths of less immediate importance were reserved for the scientific research of future ages.

Another difficulty much more serious than those noted above now demands attention. In Gen. ii. 17 we read: "In the day that thou eatest thereof, thou shalt surely die." The fulfilment of this threat is asserted in 1 Cor. xv. 22: "In Adam all die." And it is made the basis of an important argument in Rom. v. 12–19. This argument is a plain assertion by the most conspicuous of the early followers of Christ that the universal reign of death over man is a result of Adam's first sin. On the other hand, it must be admitted that long before Adam lived multitudes of animals died. And the close relation between the bodily structure of men and animals leaves no room for doubt that the death of the one stands in close relation to the death of the other. Thus the assured results of modern science seem to contradict the theology of Paul.

This apparent contradiction, considered as an objection to the teaching of the Apostle, will be sufficiently removed if I can suggest a plausible hypothesis in harmony with each of the apparently conflicting statements. For the objection assumes that they cannot be harmonized.

We have already found reason to believe that the intelligence and the moral sense of man were not produced by the operation of natural forces but by the inbreathing of a higher life into a body closely related to the bodies of animals. Only thus can we account for the impassable line separating the lowest men from the highest animals. If so, we can well conceive the Author of this higher life promising to His new-born creature, man, that if he were loyal to the guidance of this new and nobler life he should escape from the doom of death to which all lower animals were subject. Certainly, He who was able to breathe into bodily form this spiritual life was able to guard it, even in a body of flesh, from the stroke of death. And I may venture to suggest, in view of the close relation between men and animals, that, had man been faithful in his day of trial, his victory would possibly have re-acted on the animal kingdom and have rescued it from its ancient doom. Man obeyed the impulses he had in common with animals; and thus sank to their level of mortality.

The above suggestion is little more than speculation. But it rests on a basis as broad as that of the objection we are now considering. And it shows that the universal reign of death in the geologic ages is not necessarily inconsistent with the theological teaching of Paul.

The story of the flood has received remarkable confirmation from the traditions of many nations, even those most widely separated. For the similarity of these traditions, amid differences in detail, reveals their common origin; and proves that, as matter of fact, before its wide dispersion the whole race perished, with the exception of one family which escaped in a floating vessel, by a catastrophe of water. These traditions, a common heirloom, bear silent but indisputable witness to the unity of the human race.

Looking at the whole case, our chief wonder is the absence, even from the Old Testament, of serious collision with the findings of modern science. The one epistle of Clement of Rome contains a story, that of the Phœnix in ch. xxv., far more unworthy of a place in a sacred book than any in the Bible. For the absence of such absurdities, the Christian may well thank that Unseen Hand which guided and guarded the writers and compilers and editors of his Sacred Books.

V.

Biblical Rationalism.

The above title I have used to designate a school of thought which endeavours to explain the indisputable facts of Christianity apart from any outward events essentially different from the ordinary course of the material world. It is thus closely related to, though as we shall see widely differing from, Scientific Agnosticism, which endeavours to explain all phenomena by the operation of the forces at work in inorganic matter.

Agnosticism, inasmuch as it denies or refuses to acknowledge the supernatural, necessarily implies a rationalistic explanation of the facts of Christianity. And such explanations, some Agnostics are eager to bring forward. But Rationalists are by no means necessarily Agnostics. For a man may have an assured belief in the existence of an intelligent Creator and Ruler of the world, and in exact retribution beyond the grave, and yet deny that Christ rose from the dead. Consequently, Rationalism admits many shades of opinion from pronounced Materialism to sincere worship of a Father in heaven. But all Rationalists believe that Jesus was the Greatest of men. And many of them believe that He stood in a unique relation to God, that in Him God came nearer to man than ever before or since, and that consequently there was in Him a Life immeasurably higher than the ordinary life of men. But all Rationalists agree to deny, not only that Christ rose from the dead, but that there was in Him a Personality older than the universe and distinct from the Father; and that the need for His death as a means of salvation from sin lay in the justice of God.

Among Rationalists popularly known I may mention Strauss and Renan. Far abler than these was Ferdinand Baur (A.D. 1792–1860), founder of the Tübingen school. Other well-known names are Keim, Pfleiderer, Zeller, Holtzmann, Hausrath. Also to the Old Testament have Rationalist scholars paid great attention. Conspicuous among them now are Kuenen and Wellhausen.

The general conception of Rationalists about the origin of Christianity, I shall best reproduce by giving some account of the opinions of a modern representative. For this purpose I select a writer of accurate New Testament scholarship, fairness, and reverence, Dr. Pfleiderer of Berlin. From his pen we have a work entitled *Paulinism*, reproducing fairly and fully the teaching of Paul; a *Philosophy of Religion*, tracing the development, contents, and operation, of the religious consciousness; and a more recent work, *Original Christianity, its Writings and*

Teaching,[1] giving an account of the various documents and various types of teaching found in the New Testament.

Pfleiderer denies the possibility of miracles. He reminds us[2] that "the other historical religions have their miraculous legends as well as Christianity, the person of the founder and the early spread of the religion being in every instance adorned with them;" and complains that modern Christianity is illogical because it "considers its own miracles (ecclesiastical or at least Biblical) to be historically true, but those of the other religions to be mere tales and legends." Unfortunately, he does not define the word *miracle*; but suggests a meaning by speaking about "the interruptions of the connexion of nature," of "a violation of the order of nature and a breach of law," of the intellect asserting "an inviolable and constant order of the world according to its inner laws," of "miracle viewed as an occurrence contrary to order," of "phenomena contrary to law," of "miracle proper" as being "the suspension of law;" adding, "of a contradiction of the universal law, a breaking through the natural connexion of cause and effect, there is nowhere a trace in such cases, and we cannot apply to them the term of 'miracle' in the absolute sense." It will be observed that in the argument of this lecture the word *miracle* is not used. And I have endeavoured to show that the resurrection of Christ is no more a violation of the order of nature or breach of law than is the diversion of a sunbeam by the leaf of a tree. And we saw that, although the resurrection

---

[1] *Das Urchristenthum, seine Schriften und Lehren.*
[2] *Philosophy of Religion.* vol. iv. p. 85.

of the dead was a diversion of natural forces such as we never see now, it was no more so than was the first arrangement of atoms into organic chemical compounds and of the resulting molecules into living cells involved in the origin of life. Consequently, Pfleiderer's argument against miracles has no force against the resurrection of Christ as here expounded. But he takes for granted that it is decisive. And, when discussing the origin of Christianity, he assumes, as needing no further proof and indeed as almost self-evident, that Christ did not rise from the dead.

The baselessness of this fundamental inference, I have in Section vii. endeavoured to show. Surely there is nothing inconsistent with the order of nature or with the character of God in the belief that at certain great epochs He breathed into inorganic matter and then into lost humanity a new life. For, in each case, the development of the new life was in harmony with the order already existing. Certainly, the inconsistency is as great in the one case as the other.

Having in the work just quoted set aside miracle as impossible, our author goes on in his *Original Christianity* to trace, by a careful study of the Christian documents, the rise of the Christian Church. He admits as genuine the Epistles to the Romans, Corinthians, Galatians, 1 Thessalonians, and Philippians. Of the Four Gospels, he considers the Second to be the earliest. " It is the first attempt which has reached us to represent, in the narrative form of a history of the life and suffering of Jesus, the Gospel of Jesus as the Christ, which Paul had announced as theological teaching. As certainly as in this narrative the oldest materials of traditions have been worked up, so clearly is there revealed the influence, determining the conception of details, of the great teacher Paul, whose personal disciple the composer of the oldest Gospel apparently was."[1] He sees[2] "nothing against, and everything for, the correctness of the ecclesiastical tradition" that the Second Gospel was written by John Mark the companion of Paul. But he believes our present copies to have been interpolated. The First Gospel he supposes to be later than, and dependent upon, the Second and Third, and to be "a harmonizing combination of the same in the interest of the Church; and that it was written in the second century, and more likely in its third than its second decade." The Book of Acts he accepts as by the author of the Third Gospel. The Epistles to the Colossians and Ephesians, he considers to be later products of the school of Paul; and the Fourth Gospel to have been written between A.D. 135 and 150, (i.e. about the time of the birth of Irenæus,) under the influence of followers of Paul. That Irenæus remembered Polycarp speaking about his recollections of the Apostle John, to whom with complete confidence Irenæus attributes this document, makes this last suggestion very unlikely.

Dr. Pfleiderer admits that "the Christian community arose out of wonderful experiences of the first disciples of Jesus, from which they gained the certainty that the crucified Jesus had risen and was alive." He goes on to say that the accounts in the Gospels are so contradictory that they give no definite conception; and that it is impossible to conceive "a body of the Risen One which at one time like an earthly body can be touched and can eat, and at another time seems to be of superhuman kind because it

---

[1] Pfleiderer's *Ur-Christenthum*, p. 360.   [2] *Ibid.* p. 414.

goes through closed doors, suddenly appears and vanishes, and is taken up to heaven."

Having thus set aside as inconceivable and impossible the actual resurrection of Christ, Pfleiderer goes on to explain, without it, the origin of Christianity. He finds a clue in Christ's quotation in Mark xiv. 28 of the words of Zech. xiii. 7, "The sheep shall be scattered," taken in connexion with the words recorded in Mark xvi. 7, "He goeth before you into Galilee." All this our author takes as an indication that after the crucifixion the dismayed disciples fled to their Northern homes; that there, removed from the scene of the crucifixion and amid scenes redolent with memories of Jesus, the deep impression He had made upon them returned with full force and assured them that such a teacher could not be destroyed by death. Already they were familiar with the idea of resurrection of the dead. Under such circumstances, Pfleiderer conceives that some one, probably Peter, fancied that he had seen the Lord. The belief spread, became general among the scattered disciples, and took the form of a belief that Christ had risen from the dead. The Galileans went as usual to the feast of weeks at Jerusalem. There, on the Day of Pentecost, a company of them assembled. Naturally they thought and spoke about Him who only seven weeks before, at the last great festival, had been cruelly murdered. Enthusiasm was raised to the highest point. Peter boldly proclaimed to a crowd outside that the murdered One was in very truth the hoped-for Deliverer, and that He had risen from the dead. His words were believed: and on that day thousands were added to the company of the followers of the Crucified. The vision of

Paul on the way to Damascus, like the other appearances, is supposed by Pfleiderer[1] to be, as to its form if not altogether, subjective. From these imaginations resulted the early Christian Church and the mighty influence which has changed the entire current of human history.

The mention in each of the Four Gospels of events at the tomb of Christ on the morning after the Sabbath, and in the Third and Fourth Gospels of appearances to the disciples at Jerusalem, our author considers to be later traditions prompted by desire to save the fame of the Apostles from the disgrace of having run away to Galilee while their Master lay dead in the grave. But of such jealousy for the fame of the Apostles there is no trace elsewhere in the Gospels. Certainly nothing is done to shield the reputation of an illustrious Apostle who is reported to have denied his Master with oaths and curses.

Pfleiderer admits that in Paul's view the death of Christ was an atonement for the sins of the world, an atonement demanded by the Law of God. "The purpose of the sending of Christ in the flesh, Paul sees not in the earthly life of Jesus, but in His death; with this together with the resurrection is linked exclusively, in his view, the entire redeeming salvation-work of Christ. The death of Christ was, according to Paul, redemptive for this reason, because, as the atonement appointed by God for the sins of the world, He removed the religious misery of the consciousness of guilt and the moral bondage of the service of the Law, and brought about the blessedness and freedom of being children of God. This is the constant teaching of

[1] *Orig. Christianity*, p. 39.

Paul about the redemption work of Christ."[1] Our author admits also that Paul believed in the pre-existence of Christ. Referring to 2 Cor. viii. 9, he says, "The wealth which He in kindness to us gave up at His entrance into the poverty of His earthly life consisted in the heavenly glory which He, as image and splendour of God, possessed in the heavenly pre-existence."[2] And he says again and again that Paul's faith in Christ and devotion to Christ rested upon his firm belief that Christ had risen from the dead.

In general agreement with Pfleiderer is Keim's very able and instructive *History of Jesus of Nazara*. But the differences in critical detail are many: *e.g.* he considers Matthew[3] to be the earliest, and Mark the latest, of the Synoptist Gospels; and places the Fourth Gospel at the beginning of the second century.[4] Keim admits the high character and intelligence of Paul and the firm belief of him and the other Apostles that Christ rose from the dead. But in this he supposes them to have been in error. A bodily resurrection, he dismisses[5] as inconceivable.

Keim discusses, and says much in favour of, the vision theory expounded above. But he points out with great fairness its inadequacy to explain the facts of the case.[6] Especially he calls attention to the early and sudden cessation of the visions, attested by a reliable witness.[7] He then states his own position. "All these considerations compel us to admit that the theory which has recently become the favourite one is only an hypothesis

---

[1] *Ur-Christenthum*, p. 222.   [2] *Ibid.* p. 217.
[3] *Jesus of Nazara*, vol. i. p. 69.   [4] *Ibid.* p. 223.
[5] *Ibid.* vi. p. 339.   [6] *Ibid.* pp. 351 ff.
[7] 1 Cor. xv. 1-10.

which, while it explains something, leaves the main fact unexplained, and indeed subordinates what is historically attested to weak and untenable views. But if the attempt to retain the traditional theory of the resurrection miscarries, as well as the undertaking to construct a natural explanation of what occurred by the help of the Pauline visions, then nothing remains but to admit that the mythical character of the detailed narratives, and the obscure brevity of what is credible in the history, do not enable us to arrive at a certain and incontestable result concerning the mysterious events that closed the life of Jesus, weighty as they are in themselves and influential as they have been in the history of the world. For history, which reckons only with concrete numbers and with sequences of tangible, recognised causes and effects, there exists as factual and unquestionable simply the belief of the Apostles that Jesus rose again, with the immense result of that belief, the Christianizing of mankind. This was the position taken up by Hegel, and afterwards by Baur; and it is to their modest, sober, common-sense position that we must return from the vaunted explanatory suppositions."

Keim holds firmly that in Jesus Christ God came near to man, in a way altogether unique, in order to bless and to save him. He also believes that the supposed appearances of Jesus were not mere subjective imaginations, but were produced in men by an actual and objective, though spiritual and incorporeal, revelation from God; that in spirit Jesus returned to earth and showed Himself to His disciples, producing in them a well-grounded assurance that the Crucified still lives with God. He believes that, but for this spiritual appearance, the work of Jesus, "which was to affect the history of the world, would have been ruined by the disastrous death of the Messiah.... All evidences go to prove that the belief in the Messiah would have died out without the living Jesus; and by the return of the Apostles to the synagogue, to Judaism, the gold of the words of Jesus would have been buried in the dust of oblivion." [1]

The above theory recognises a direct and supernatural revelation from God to man in Jesus Christ, and a life beyond death. It thus rises immensely above the Agnostic position which ignores the supernatural, the unseen, and the eternal. But it contradicts the firm belief of Paul. For he distinguishes clearly between his own visions, *e.g.* Acts xxvi. 19, 2 Cor. xii. 1, and the one historic fact of the bodily resurrection of Christ which took place on the third day (1 Cor. xv. 4) and was attested by subsequent visions.

Keim agrees with Pfleiderer in believing that Paul and all the various writers of the New Testament were altogether in error in ascribing to Christ a pre-existent and divine personality distinct from that of the Father, and in ascribing to His death a definite relation to the justice of God. Each of these writers places the real worth of the work of Christ in His moral teaching, in His assertion of the Fatherhood of God, and in His example.

Very interesting is the account of Jesus and of the origin of Christianity given by the learned Jewish writer Graetz in his *History of the Jews*. He admits that Jesus of Nazareth has made universal the knowledge of God which

---

[1] *History of Jesus of Nazara*, vol. vi. 363 f.

till His day had been confined to the Jewish nation; and agrees with the above writers in saying that the faith of the Apostles rested upon their confident belief that Christ rose from the dead. This confidence he endeavours to explain by supposing that in some mysterious way Jesus had performed remarkable cures of bodily disease.[1] He thus admits that the Apostles' faith in the Crucified was such as could not be accounted for by any ordinary course of events.

The rationalistic hypothesis discussed above implies that Jesus was grossly misunderstood by all His early followers, even by those who have secured for Him the veneration of the whole civilised world during all succeeding ages; and that they attributed to Him claims from which He would have shrunk back with horror as blasphemous. On this hypothesis, Paul did for Christ that which His enemies accused Him of doing for Himself: "Thou being a man makest Thyself God."[2] And Paul and his companion Apostles are "found out" by modern scientific criticism to be unwittingly "false witnesses of God, because" they "have borne witness against God that He raised Christ, whom He did not raise."[3] Yet Keim admits that Paul saved the work of Christ from failure and the name of Christ from comparative oblivion; and that Christ has changed the whole course of human history and saved the world.

Strange to say, according to the theory before us, the serious error which led astray the early followers of Christ has in recent days been detected. And, stranger

[1] *Geschichte der Juden*, 4th ed. vol. iii. p. 296.
[2] John x. 33.   [3] 1 Cor. xv. 15.

still, the discovery of the truth has, apparently, added nothing to the moral influence of Christianity.

The School of Thought represented by Keim and Pfleiderer claims to be historic. It is now evident that it rejects as unhistoric all the Christian documents; and does this, not for historic reasons, but because certain conspicuous statements in them conflict with a scientific theory, viz. that all material phenomena in the past were an outworking of the natural forces now seen in operation. This theory, I have in Section vii. already discussed.

It would be unjust to close this note without acknowledging the many and great services to Christian truth rendered by the School of Biblical Rationalism. In all ages the Church of Christ has bowed with reverence before the divine truth embodied in Holy Scripture. But for the more part the halo of reverence has somewhat obscured the human clothing of this superhuman revelation. The writers before us, by directing special attention to this human element, to the languages, to the logical arguments and trains of thought, to the different types of teaching, and to the entire historic surroundings of the Bible, have done much to elucidate its meaning, and thus to lay a foundation for a broader and more accurate knowledge of the divine truth revealed in Jesus Christ and embodied in the Sacred Volume.

www.ingramcontent.com/pod-product-compliance
Lightning Source LLC
Chambersburg PA
CBHW020911230426
43666CB00008B/1405